Noticed, But Not Seen

Noticed, But Not Seen

Norm Sawyer

Norm Sawyer

© 2022 Norm Sawyer
ISBN 10: 1-988226-54-6
ISBN 13: 978-1-988226-54-5
Cover art: Kane Sawyer
Cover graphics: Lee MacLennan
Black and white photos: Norm Sawyer

Published by

First Page Publishing
Kelowna, BC, Canada

DEDICATION

This book is dedicated with a special thanks to my publisher, Clay Kessler, who trusts my writing.

Scott Moore, my editor, whose friendship keeps my writing honest.

Jami Rogers, my editor, whose encouragement helps me try again.

CONTENTS

FOREWORD

I am a manager of a substance-controlled facility. I have seen firsthand the hurt that 'Being noticed but not seen' causes. Looking into people's eyes and truly seeing them—not only for who they are, but who they can become—is a gift. Being a busy mom of five, the tasks and roles I daily fulfill are often unseen, and the reminder that I work for an audience of One is an amazing privilege. We all fill roles that are often unseen by many, but always seen by a gracious God.

I first met Norm in 1999. It was in a class I audited through the Bible College at Kelowna Christian Centre. I was an energetic, impressionable young lass eager to learn. I definitely learned in his class, and grew to trust Norm: his pursuit for truth, his passion for God, and his love for people. He inspired me to think out of the box in my faith. Little did I know that this out-of-the-box thinker would play such a huge part of my healing in my early forties.

When struggling in February 2020, his

name came to mind when I reached a point of desperation in my health. From our first meeting, I knew that our paths were spirit-led and God-driven. The renewal of not only my physical health, but also my spiritual and emotional health, has been long and hard. Norm's books have been a huge part of my journey. At times, his writings have been a gentle nudge, a push; and at times, a full body slam towards God.

In this book, Norm demonstrates what it means to be a spirit-filled Christian in a broken world. It serves as a tool for making the Word of God relatable and relevant. Norm shares his life, his struggles and his personal experiences in a raw and powerful way. His communication is both challenging and authentic, providing empowering truths about God and how He is the answer every time—regardless of what the question is.

Through meeting with Norm monthly, he has been my mentor, coach, and pastor, and I have found an unlikely friend. I have benefitted from his wisdom, discernment, perspective and genuine care for people. In this book, I know you will see and feel the same. It is no accident that you are holding this book in your hands.

Noticed, But Not Seen

As you read it, may each word remind you that you are seen by the Creator of all things, the all-knowing God, and that you are loved beyond measure. May this book serve as a guide in your quest for truth and healing.

Blessings,
Elaine Gonzales

Norm Sawyer

PART ONE:

SEEING OURSELVES

Noticed, But Not Seen

Seeing ourselves through the eyes of God can change the way we see ourselves through the eyes and opinions of others. Our faith must be in who God says we are and not who the world says we are. 1John 4:16 So we have come to know and to believe the love that God has for us. God is love, and whoever abides in love abides in God, and God abides in him.

NOTICED, BUT NOT SEEN

Proverbs 3:28 If you can help your neighbor now, don't say, "Come back tomorrow, and then I'll help you."

As I walk by the homeless man on the street, I notice him, but I do not see him for who he is, or who he was before he became homeless. I do not see the fact that he has a mother, maybe a sister or even children. I only see the shell of a person who is begging and gazing out to nowhere with the thousand-yard stare. I'm sure he once had dreams and ambitions that somehow lost meaning along the way. Who's to say he still does not have goals or a dream of getting off of the street. Maybe I could find out for sure if I stopped and talked with him, but as I walk by him, I only notice his shabbiness and clearly, I do not see his heart. We tend to notice the homeless, but we do not see them or their plight.

Lately, we are seeing the native Indigenous population in Canada because so many unmarked graves have been discovered. This atrocity is pointing out to the world what the First Nations people have always known - the barbarity of our historic and present legislative decisions has only caused this segment of society to be noticed but not seen as a people. However, after discovering numerous unmarked graves that the native population knew were always there, we are now seeing these people. Hopefully, we can honestly be reconciled in spirit and in truth and not just offer platitudes and clichés of "We have to try harder, blah blah blah." Prov. 3:28 **If you can help your neighbor now, don't say, "Come back tomorrow, and then I'll help you."**

If it was not for the pandemic, it would not have been revealed how terrible we have been treating our elderly by stuffing them away in poorly governed care homes. We would have continued to just notice the elderly and not see them the way the Lord sees them. Psalm 92:14 **Even in old age they will still produce fruit; they will remain vital and green.** Even though the word of the Lord says the elderly will bear fruit in old age, our solipsistic lifestyles have no room for those who are elderly and who are in need. Maybe now that we have seen them, we can improve on the way we take care of them.

At some time in our life, we have all experienced being noticed but not seen for who we truly are. Some people feel like a non-person as they plod along in life. The people who feel they are living a nonexistent life will have to decide in their hearts to make an effort to see and acknowledge others who are feeling the same way they do. If we want friends, we have to extend a hand of friendship. We do reap what we sow. We will have to sow some honest effort into seeing others if we want to be seen. We will have to push through the haze of life and see others rather than just notice the crowds. If you are lonely then reach out to the lonely. If you are depressed then reach out to those who are suffering the same sadness. Luke 6:38a **Give, and it shall be given unto you.**

There is hope. Our God knows exactly where we are on the world map. James 1:1b **To the twelve tribes scattered among the nations: Greetings.** He knows our address and our situation. The Lord sees us for who He made us to be in Him. Some people may feel like they are neither noticed nor seen, but rest assured, our heavenly Father is looking at us individually right now, and planning our future. The Lord knows us intimately. Jer. 29:11 **For I know the plans I have for you," says the LORD. "They are plans for good and not for disaster, to give you a future and a hope."** God sees all our situations throughout our whole life. Psalm 121:8 **The LORD keeps watch over you as you come and go, both now and forever.** To the Lord, we are never nonexistent nor a non-person. We are His chosen creation.

As I get older in years, I hope that I can mature in my heart where I see my fellow man the way the Lord sees them rather than just notice them. It would be impossible to see everyone on earth, however, we can start by seeing our children and finding out what is on their hearts. We can begin to see our neighbours, cashiers at the stores we frequent, and those we come in contact with regularly. We can sincerely ask the people in the church assemblies we attend, "How their souls are holding up during these difficult days." Taking the time to see the other people God created will help us see ourselves for who we truly are. May we rise to the challenge that is set before us and begin to see. God have mercy on us.

THE BOOK OF LOOPHOLES

Proverbs 30:5 Every word of God is flawless; He is a shield to those who take refuge in Him.

Charles Spurgeon said, "We shall not adjust our Bible to the age; but before we have done with it, by God's grace, we shall adjust the age to the Bible."

As I was reading my bible or The Book Of Loopholes as it is sometimes used in that way, I was struck by the fact that I caught myself looking in the scriptures for a way out of doing something God asked me to do, rather than being humbled that God asked me to do something for Him. Why is it, when I am walking right with the Lord, the illuminated word of the Bible becomes a lamp for my steps in life and a light to make the road ahead clear to see? Psalm 119:105 **Your word is a lamp to my feet and a light to my path.** However, when I am falling into an area of sin, then the convicting word of the Bible becomes the book of loopholes that I am using to try and justify my poor choices. I find myself using the same book in two entirely different ways.

As the Apostle Paul said in exasperation, "Oh the wretched man that I am." Rom. 7:24 **Oh, what a miserable person I am! Who will free me from this life that is dominated by sin and death?** If we are going to participate in stretching the truth to suit our moods, then we are setting ourselves up for disappointment. Self-deception can be worse than being deceived by Satan because when the deception has been fully exposed, there is an added feeling of stupidity on top of the shame and guilt Satan is accusing us of. Then we beat ourselves up with accusing questions of "Why of my own free will, did I do these stupid things? It was clearly a bonehead thing to do, and yet, I talked myself into this mess." Prov. 14:12 **There is a way that appears to be right, but in the end it leads to death.**

Within the human race, there is a tendency to try and save ourselves. The fact is that Jesus is the only saviour who can wash away our sins and create within us a new heart of praise for the Lord. As Jesus said, "You cannot patch up old garments with a new cloth," There has to be an entirely different way of getting the real results

God wants in our life. Mark 2:21 **No one sews a patch of unshrunk cloth on an old garment. Otherwise, the new piece will pull away from the old, making the tear worse.** We often think we have a new idea to fix our old problems but as the scripture says the method of repair has to be a whole new way of getting our souls and hearts healed. It cannot be the same old thing packaged as a new cure. It has to be God's way of doing things and His way is through Christ. It is not a patchwork of our own doing, it is a clean and holy finished work of the Lord's doing.

It does not matter the cleverness a person puts into searching the word of God to make it say what the reader wants it to say. The loopholes are not there. The interpretation of what is there can be made to become a loophole, but at the end of all the mental wrangling and carnal invention pursuing this vanity, the word of the Lord speaks plainly. It does not say, "Thou shalt not steal between the hours of." It says, "Thou shalt not steal!" The word of the Lord does not imply, "You shall not bear false witness against your neighbour unless he is with the Republican party." No, it says, "You shall not bear false witness against your neighbour." There are no loopholes to suit your personal bias and judgments unless you make them up. Prov. 30:5 **Every word of God is flawless; He is a shield to those who take refuge in Him.**

There is a story in the book of Daniel where the magicians, governors, and princes of Babylon were trying to destroy Daniel because of the favour Daniel had with King Darius. The schemers concluded the only way to attack Daniel was through the law of his God. They produced a plan that would appeal to King Darius' ego - that no one in the kingdom could make a prayerful request for anything to a man or God. Only the king himself could be petitioned for thirty days. Dan. 6:8 **And now, Your Majesty, issue and sign this law so it cannot be changed, an official law of the Medes and Persians that cannot be revoked.** However, Daniel continued to pray three times a day and give thanks to the Lord.

Daniel was reported to the king for praying to God, and now, the king had to act on the law that was unchangeable. There were no loopholes for the king to use to deliver Daniel, and therefore,

Daniel was lowered into the lion's den. The king was overjoyed when he found out the next day that the true God had delivered Daniel. We have to be careful in creating doctrines and rules to suit personal bias, because as the magicians and governors found out - that by creating a scheme that had no grace for Daniel, also had no grace for the same jealous people who had plotted a vengeful ruse. Dan. 6:24 **Then the king gave orders to arrest the men who had maliciously accused Daniel. He had them thrown into the lions' den, along with their wives and children. The lions leaped on them and tore them apart before they even hit the floor of the den.**

The word of God is a light for my life's righteous journey and not a book of loopholes to ingratiate my whims. Like the magicians and governors, the loopholes that are looked for to have our own way can come back to damage the real relationship that we have with God. Yes, God is always there to love and heal us, even from our own stupidity, but why make it harder on ourselves than it has to be? Why look outside of God's holy leading? Why look for loopholes, isn't God's grace enough? Isa. 59:1 **Listen! The LORD's arm is not too weak to save you, nor is his ear too deaf to hear you call.** Yes, saints, God is more than enough. Amen!

PUBLIC OPINION

Proverbs 17:13 Whoever rewards evil for good, evil will not depart from his house.

At the beginning of the pandemic, public opinion had our courageous nurses at the top of the popularity meter. However, within a short time, the same public opinion group was protesting and cursing these same overworked, vulnerable, and tired health servants. This obnoxious public voice was trying to make our nurses the new social outcasts that we are supposed to hate. If these same protesters had been born two thousand years earlier, they would have been the ones shouting, "Hosanna" as Jesus rode a donkey into the city of Jerusalem, only to turn around and scream, "Crucify Him" days later. Public opinion can be fickle and cruel.

Since when have we, as a society, modelled our lives to the standards of public opinion? How did the gospel of public opinion become the go-to training manual for living in this scornful world? The cesspool of thought that public opinion contains is an offensive stench that has no value for establishing any integral standard of good living practices. The mercurial nature of public opinion is in itself unable to find any level of forthright behaviour because it sways with the voice of discontent and the confusion of dysfunction. Public opinion's foundations are nothing more than toxic slurry and quicksand, resulting in a dark mass of ugliness.

Mark Twain said, "A lie can travel around the world and back again while the truth is lacing up its boots." Online statistics (if they can be trusted) state that conspiracy theories and lies that public opinion is built upon will spread six times faster on social media platforms than the truth will. This would also explain why there is no way these online web giants are going to stop this type of online posting because it is such a large part of their revenue stream. Every level of government can drag all the CEOs of these mega-web platform companies before all kinds of congressional panels and grill the life out of them, and still, it will make no difference to the content posted. There is just too much money to be made with online falsities. Prov. 17:13

Whoever rewards evil for good, evil will not depart from his house.

Why is it easier to believe the fabrications of public opinion than the truth? I believe the truth often contains a moral substance that can be hard to follow, and since the character of mankind is weak and sinfully flawed, the lie is easier to digest, even though it tastes bad. Rom. 1:24a **So God abandoned them to do whatever shameful things their hearts desired.** Therefore, we have to become the gatekeepers to what we allow into our hearts. We should be asking the Holy Spirit what the truth of the matter is so that we can proceed in confidence.

If we are to overcome the storms and influences of public opinion, we are going to have to become secure in our souls by being established on the solid ground of God's word. The only solid foundation that does not buckle under pressure is the ground held by the Rock of Ages. Jesus said that we should build our house on a rock so we could weather the storms of life and every lie that the world throws at us. Matt. 7:24 **Therefore, everyone who hears these words of mine and acts on them will be like**

a wise man who built his house on the rock.

Wisdom is building our lives on what God says rather than unproven conspiracies. Eph. 4:14 **Then we will no longer be little children, tossed by the waves and blown around by every wind of teaching, by human cunning with cleverness in the techniques of deceit.** God has never lied to us and never will. It is not in His character nor His heart to do so. Jesus said that He is the truth, and truth acted upon will set us free. If you have aligned yourself with a false public belief that has bound your mind and heart, then it is time to seek the truth and be set free to become who God created you to be. John 8:32 **And you will know the truth, and the truth will set you free.**

We were not created to become a mouthpiece for the lies the enemy has promoted in this life. We are not to encourage the vitriol of public opinion. We are to be a voice of wisdom and calm in the turbulent storms that are taking place in this world. Let us bring the wisdom of the Holy Spirit into the harshness that surrounds us on all sides. God's truth and blessing be upon us all. Amen!

I HAVE THE ANSWER

Proverbs 15:6 In the house of the righteous is much treasure: but in the revenues of the wicked is trouble.

I was talking with a brother in the Lord who was excited that he was headed out of town and Province to see a well-known healing-evangelist. He said he was going to get hands laid on him so he could be healed. I asked him if he had asked any of our elders or prayer team within our assembly to pray for him. He looked at me with some confusion and said, "Do any of them have a healing ministry?" I said, "The word of God says we should ask the elders to pray." James 5:14 **Is any sick among you? let him call for the elders of the church; and let them pray over him, anointing him with oil in the name of the Lord: 15 And the prayer of faith shall save the sick, and the Lord shall raise him up; and if he have committed sins, they shall be forgiven him.**

Please don't get me wrong. I was not trying

to stop him from his trip to get healed, on the contrary, I was trying to help him get healed right on the spot. I love the gifts within the body of Christ and the more healing-evangelists the better; however, at that moment in time I was thinking of the words my wife often says, "The answer is in the house." What she is saying is that the answer or anything we need right then and there can be sought within the church body. There is always something in our possession or someone praying that can take care of our needs. I have found that my wife's conviction in this idea to be a reality. I am blessed to have often found the answer within our spiritual environment where there is always someone who will pray or step up to help.

One of the amazing things about the body of Christ is the diversity of ministry and the individuality of people working in submission to God who can help through ministry, service, or supply for any situation. Joel 2:27 **And ye shall know that I am in the midst of Israel, and that I am the LORD your God, and none else: and my people shall never be ashamed.** How often have we wondered, how is God going to get the miracle to me in time? How is He even going to pull it off? We look for things that are often found right under our noses, and I find this to be a truth in my spiritual walk as well.

When Moses was trying to explain his distressful situation to God, whether the enslaved Hebrews would believe that God had sent him, God simply responded with these words. Ex. 4:2 **And the LORD said unto him, What is that in thine hand? And he said, A rod. 17 And thou shalt take this rod in thine hand, wherewith thou shalt do signs.** Moses did not have to look far for the answer, because the answer was in his hand.

When the widow asked Elisha for his help to get out of a difficult situation 2Kings 4:1 **Now there cried a certain woman of the wives of the sons of the prophets unto Elisha, saying, Thy servant my husband is dead; and you know that thy servant did fear the LORD: and the creditor is come to take unto him my two sons to be bondmen.** Elisha asked the widow a few simple questions. 2Kings 4:2 **And Elisha said unto her, What shall I do for thee? tell me, what hast thou in the house? And she said, Thine handmaid hath not any thing in**

the house, save a pot of oil. The instruction that Elisha gave the widow was within her capability and neighbourhood. She was instructed to borrow vessels from her neighbours, close the door and fill the vessels with oil, then sell the oil to get out of debt and live off of the rest. The answer for her and her sons was literally, "In the house."

Prov. 15:6a **In the house of the righteous is much treasure.** If we are His righteousness, then the answer is very close and within reach. We read of a scribe who had asked Jesus what was the first commandment of all. Jesus gave this scribe a heartfelt satisfactory answer. Mark 12:32 **And the scribe said unto him, Well, Master, thou hast said the truth.** Then Jesus says to the scribe that his answer was close to reaching the Kingdom of God. Mark 12:34a **And when Jesus saw that he answered discreetly, he said unto him, Thou art not far from the kingdom of God.** I can almost hear Jesus whisper to the scribe's soul, "As a matter of fact, you are looking at the Kingdom maker." Jesus is not only the King of the Kingdom, but everything the Kingdom of God represents. The answer for this scribe was within reach of touching the creator of all.

I would encourage all of us to use the five-fold ministry gifts that God has given to the church for the perfecting and building up of all Christians. Eph. 4:11 **And he gave some, apostles; and some, prophets; and some, evangelists; and some, pastors and teachers; 12 For the perfecting of the saints, for the work of the ministry, for the edifying of the body of Christ.** The answer is in the word of God. The answer is in the body of Christ, so let us take care of each other so we can manifest the glory of God through His written word that clearly pronounces our victory in Christ. What is in your hand, or sphere of influence? Work with it and see what God can do. Blessings on us all.

BE REDEEMED

Proverbs 3:5 Trust in the LORD with all thine heart; and lean not unto thine own understanding.

Why do movies that tell stories about redemption do so well at the box office? The reasons are many, but the underlying fact is that everyone is looking for redemption and it has already been given to us.

Why do we not accept the redemption that God offers through Christ His Son? It might be the deep-seated feelings of guilt and the unreasonable belief that we have to pay for the wrong or sin that put us in the place of needing redemption in the first place. What a vicious circle. We want and need redemption, but we want to redeem ourselves our own way. Prov. 14:12 **There is a way which seems right unto a man, but the end thereof are the ways of death.**

The word of the Lord is clear that God's way is the only way. John 14:6 **Jesus saith unto him, I am the way, the truth, and the life: no man comes unto the Father, but by me.** Acts 4:12

Neither is there salvation in any other: for there is none other name under heaven given among men, whereby we must be saved. Even though we know these verses to be true in our heart of hearts, we still try to cover up and redeem ourselves from all the messes we end up in. After a long attempt at failing in our own way of redemption, we finally call on God to deliver us. Lam. 3:58 **O Lord, thou hast pleaded the causes of my soul; thou hast redeemed my life.** The process is long and arduous, but we do it anyway.

The beauty about the finished redemptive work of Christ is that everything has already been done that will ever have to be done. Gal. 3:13 **Christ hath redeemed us from the curse of the law, being made a curse for us: for it is written, Cursed is every one that hangs on a tree.** There is no more need for fig-leaf religion; Christ has redeemed us. This is past tense and it is done.

What do we do when we find ourselves starting to act out our redemption our own way after we have sinned? First, realise that the sin just committed has been paid for in full and, by faith, repent then and there. 1John 1:9 **If we confess our sins, he is faithful and just to forgive us our sins, and to cleanse us from all unrighteousness.**

Second, if there is still a temptation to think that there has to be some kind of self-flagellation then go, call, or text a brother or sister and pray together. James 5:16 **Confess your faults one to another, and pray one for another, that ye may be healed. The effectual fervent prayer of a righteous man avails much.**

Third, change the way we talk about ourselves and say what the word says about our redemption. Psalm 107:2 **Let the redeemed of the LORD say so, whom he hath redeemed from the hand of the enemy.**

Fourth, express gratefulness, because where there is no gratitude for what Jesus has done for us there will be no victory in anything we do. Thankfulness is the key to enjoying the redemptive work of our Lord and saviour. Gratefulness will help us be redeemed and stop us from trying to redeem ourselves. 1Thes. 5:18 **In every thing give thanks: for this is the will of God in Christ Jesus concerning you.**

Norm Sawyer

I, who have been redeemed by the finished work of Christ's gift of salvation, am grateful and I give thanks for all of you who love the Lord. Blessings.

THE WAR IS WITHIN

Proverbs 20:18 Every purpose is established by counsel: and with good advice make war.

James 4:1 **What causes quarrels and what causes fights among you? Is it not this, that your passions are at war within you?** There truly is a war within our lives that can and will tear us apart if we let it. Road rage over the smallest infractions can escalate to a court date for vehicular manslaughter. Neighbours screaming and hitting with whatever is in reach of a clenched angry hand because someone cut across a lawn. A couple of old guys in a parking lot going fisticuffs over a parking spot. The reasons for the anger in the first place may be legitimate as we have all had to deal with things people do that we do not like. However, allowing our anger to overreact in war, is a breach in our soul that exposes the true condition of our hearts. Matt. 15:19 **For from the heart come evil thoughts, murders, adulteries, sexual immoralities, thefts, false testimonies, slander.**

The counterculture protest song War performed by Edwin Starr in the 1970s still carries the same question, and the answer remains the same today, as it did back then. "War, huh, yeah. What is it good for? Absolutely nothing, uhh!" War against each other is good for nothing, but the war against the common enemy of our soul should be our full-time dedication toward destroying the works of darkness. Prov. 20:18 **Every purpose is established by counsel: and with good advice make war.** Satan has declared war on the inhabitants of the earth and has stirred up the people to focus their anger and dissatisfaction with life by fighting each other over the smallest transgressions. It is the prince of darkness we should be fighting with the weapons God has given us. 2Cor. 10:4 **The weapons we fight with are not the weapons of the world. On the contrary, they have divine power to demolish strongholds.**

The war raging within us is a result of sin that has marred our souls, causing separation from God the Father and one another. The anger and feelings of vulnerability are hyper-sensationalized by demonic powers who influence people's minds and hearts. Eph. 6:12 **For our struggle is not against flesh and blood, but against the rulers, against the authorities, against the powers of this dark world and against the spiritual forces of evil in the heavenly realms.** It is as if we are fighting a war on two fronts, one within ourselves and one with the enemy of our soul. No wonder we feel the pressure to lash out toward someone or at something. History also shows us that fighting a war on two fronts rarely results in victory. Therefore, we need a saviour who has already defeated Satan, and we need to hand over to the Lord the reasons for the warfare in our lives so that we remain victorious in Christ.

If we remain hellbent on war against everyone and everything coming our way without the leading of the Holy Spirit, we will not see the strategies against us, and we will forsake a lot of God's blessings that are available to us. We can end up turning our contrived war into an idol of personal martyrdom. Look at me, "I am the only one fighting for the church. I'm the only one God can count on," and all that rhetoric that comes out of self-righteousness. Jonah 2:8 **Those who regard and follow worthless idols**

turn away from their living source of mercy and lovingkindness.

First and foremost, we are children of peace. The war within us can be conquered with the peace of God that is available to us. Remember, Jesus, who lives within us, is the Prince of Peace. The key is to become disciplined in handing over to the Lord our choices concerning the things battling within our hearts. Yes, we are to fight by faith when God leads us into battle, however, God knows how to help us win His battles because the battle belongs to the Lord. We are not out there fighting alone. As David said to the Philistines, 1Sam. 17:47 **All those gathered here will know that it is not by sword or spear that the LORD saves; for the battle is the LORD's, and he will give all of you into our hands.** The ministry of peace is our calling, and our feet are covered in peace so that where we go, the Lord's peace comes with us. Eph. 6:15 **And with your feet fitted with the readiness that comes from the gospel of peace.**

Jesus has given us the way to fight the good fight of faith, and that is by allowing God's word to direct our lives and hearts. It is by handing over the issues that tear us apart and bring division within the church and between friends and family. The Lord has already won the war that is boiling over within people's hearts. We just have to declare a full surrender of our lives to our Saviour who loves us. Micah 4:3 **Then He will judge between many peoples and arbitrate for strong nations far and wide. Then they will beat their swords into plowshares and their spears into pruning hooks. Nation will no longer take up the sword against nation, nor will they train anymore for war.** Yes, Lord, let us walk in your peace. Amen.

THE LEAST AND THE MOST

Proverbs 28:6 Better is a poor man who walks in his integrity than a rich man who is crooked in his ways.

The thing we want the least is to die, but the thing we want the most is to be with our Lord. To get the most, we will have to eventually submit to the least thing we want. So, how do we get the most in this lifetime so that we can courageously meet the demands of the least thing wanted? The Lord teaches that we should die to ourselves while we are in this world so that we can live forever through the redemptive gift of our Lord Jesus Christ. The Apostle Paul wrote a fair amount in his epistles on the subject of dying to ourselves. Paul taught that by dying to ourselves we can live here, and eventually live eternally with our God. Phil. 1:21 **For to me to live is Christ, and to die is gain.**

Dying to self starts when we accept the gift of God's salvation through Christ. Therefore, the least we can do is realize that accepting Jesus as our Lord, is the most substantial decision we could make on this side of eternity. Dying to self is not a popular subject in a world where everyone is continually being pressured to get the most out of this commercially driven system by acquiring an endless amount of plastic ready-made stuff and limitless merchandise to become satisfied and happy. The world's message is, "Don't die to yourself, but rather, give yourself everything imaginable." However, God says to live by His spirit and not the cravings of the flesh. Rom. 8:13 **For if you live according to the flesh you will die, but if by the Spirit you put to death the deeds of the body, you will live.**

Whether it is life's momentum or of shrewd design, there is a permanent campaign at work to instill dissatisfaction within our hearts to notice what we do not have. Crowds of people are being sold a bill of goods that causes wanton cravings for whatever is deemed to be missing in their lives, and these same people end up investing their energies into the wrong areas of life to obtain fulfillment. Hag. 1:9 **You expected much, but see, it turned out to be little. What you brought home, I blew away. Why?" declares**

the LORD Almighty. "Because of my house, which remains a ruin, while each of you is busy with your own house. While chasing the most within the world, those who strive within this manner of living, end up with the least satisfaction and personal validation, because the world cannot give what is of eternal worth.

We are told by the advertising world that if we get everything we can wish for, we will live dignified lives and reach the pinnacles of pure happiness because we have everything we want. Although throughout history, this theory has proven to be wrong over and over again, we keep chasing the stuff rather than what the Lord offers us through His love. The questions we need to ask ourselves are, "Why do I need more stuff if my heart's desire is to be with the Lord? Why do I put so much emphasis on acquiring more of what the world has? How can I want what God wants for me and fulfill what I was created to do?"

It truly is a life-living balancing act to keep our eyes upon Jesus and continue paying the bills to live on this earth. This is why the joy of the Lord has to be our strength. The joy in stuff is short-lived. The joy of the Lord strengthens our souls as we walk closer with our God. Crucifying the flesh is a full-time job of faith but needed so that we are not consumed by what the flesh wants outside of God's will. Our integrity in the Lord is paramount. Prov. 28:6 **Better is a poor man who walks in his integrity than a rich man who is crooked in his ways.**

To get the most out of our lives, we will have to enter within God's narrow gateway of sanctification. It's not that the narrow gate is hard to find. On the contrary, it is clearly defined by the fact that Jesus is the gate we must walk through because He has the eternal answer for our soul. Wide is the gate that leads to the least amount of fulfilment this temporal life has to offer. Matt. 7:13 **You can enter God's Kingdom only through the narrow gate. The highway to hell is broad, and its gate is wide for the many who choose that way.** I believe the broad and wide gate is popular because there are no boundaries in the world. Anything man imagines, including sin, can walk through the broad gate and is promoted as acceptable behavior and self-righteously justified.

We who are in Christ, have the most wonderful

saviour. If you find yourself in a position of having the least amount of joy, love, and satisfaction, then give God the mess you are in, and let Him bring the most love, peace, and strength you have ever known to your heart and life. Thank you, Father, for giving us the very best of your heart. Blessings and peace be yours.

ANOTHER BITE OF THE APPLE

Proverbs 1:10 My child, if sinners entice you, turn your back on them!

I walked into the lobby of the church, and a lady who was visiting said, "Do you remember me, I was a student in your class in bible college back in 1985? When recognition dawned, I said, "Yes, I do remember you." We talked for a while concerning our lives' good and bad turning points. One of the things she said was that she had walked away from God for a time, and her life had become a mess until she repented and returned to her Lord. I have heard this story many times over the years and thought, "Why do we need another bite of the apple? Wasn't the bite of disobedience which Adam and Eve took evidence enough that life outside of God is a world of thorns and thistles?" Gen. 3:17 **To Adam he said, "Because you listened to your wife and ate fruit from the tree about which I commanded you, 'You must not eat from it,' "Cursed is the ground because of you;**

through painful toil you will eat food from it all the days of your life.

There it is, the question for all mankind. Why do we need another bite of the apple, or sinful fruit, to find out that sin still leads to death? Rom. 6:23 **For the wages of sin is death, but the gift of God is eternal life in Christ Jesus our Lord.** What is it within the heart of man that causes us to yearn for a sin that we know brings grief into our lives, and yet, we still fall into it? The human condition is in a fallen state of being, and no matter how much we try to change ourselves, we keep reaching for another bite of the apple. Our fallen nature is older than the mysteries of the Lemurian continent. Yet, we keep trying to fix ourselves with self-righteous works, which in itself, is a mystery, because we keep working at what does not work. Why do we keep hitting our heads against the wall expecting a different result, other than pain?

We see this destructive behaviour throughout the books and records of the Kings in the Old Testament. Repeatedly, the statement, "And the king did evil in the sight of the Lord," is said over and over again. King after king kept taking another bite of the apple, and it just brought more destruction upon their nation. 1Kings 15:26 **And he did evil in the sight of the LORD, and walked in the way of his father, and in his sin wherewith he made Israel to sin.** Not only did the kings keep falling for the same old things, but their disobedience allowed the people of the nation to do the same. 2Tim. 3:7 **Ever learning, and never able to come to the knowledge of the truth.**

We need to pray for our leaders because as the leadership within a country, province, or municipality is in character, the same will eventually become what people permit in their lives. What leadership allows to happen within a society will give licence to do whatever feels right, even if the activity is evil. Before you know it, many are not just taking another bite of the apple but are devouring it. Eccl. 8:11 **When the sentence for a crime is not quickly carried out, people's hearts are filled with schemes to do wrong.**

By praying for our leaders, whether you voted for them or not, we are maneuvering God's hand of conviction upon their hearts and minds. The blessing for those who do pray for their leaders is that they will live in peace, whether there is peace in the land or not. 1Tim. 2:1 **First of all, then, I urge that supplications, prayers, intercessions, and thanksgivings be made for all people, 2 for kings and all those who are in authority, so that we may lead a tranquil and quiet life in all godliness and dignity.**

The uncomprehending wonderment that is being expressed when the Psalmist says, "What is man that You are mindful of him, or the son of man that You care for him?" is truly an amazing thought. The fact that God takes such a personal interest in His creation is a mystery to behold. From the moment Adam and Eve caused a separation between God and man through disobedience, God immediately started the restoration process for mankind. Gen. 3:21 **The LORD God made garments of skin for Adam and his wife and clothed them.** From the garden of Eden, where God covered our naked shame with lambs' skins, to the cross, where the lamb of God was slain for us all, our friendship with God was reinstated. Our Heavenly Father has given His all to restore our relationship with Him and each other. We, with our free will, would be wise to graciously accept the Lord's love offering. It is the only thing we can do to become the righteousness of God in Christ and be at peace with our creator.

Before any of us consider running off and taking another bite of the apple, consider the eternal work that has been done on our behalf. For eons in the making, we have been part of a plan that is being worked out for God's eternal purpose. I realize getting our minds around this idea is somewhat perplexing from a small positional point on this earth, but we have the Mighty God living within us where His vastness of infinite power, grace, absolute loving-kindness, and wisdom resides. Is it possible that our Lord may know a bit more of the eternal plan than we do? I think so. Therefore, put away the idea of leaving God for a season just to find out that outside of the Lord's protection real death awaits us. Prov. 1:10 **My child, if sinners entice you, turn your back on them!**

The Lord is life to those who find Him and to those Jesus has found. Micah 2:7b **Do not My words do good to him who walks uprightly?** God bless you.

TEMPTATION OH TEMPTATION

Proverbs10:3 God suffers not the soul of the righteous man to famish; but he repels the craving of the wicked.

Oscar Wilde said, "I can resist anything except temptation."

It is not a sin to be tempted, it only becomes a sin when we submit to temptation and sin is born. James 1:14 **But every man is tempted, when he is drawn away of his own lust, and enticed. 15 Then when lust hath conceived, it brings forth sin: and sin, when it is finished, brings forth death.** I was asked by someone who was having a hard time with a repetitive vice, "Why does the devil keep using the same old things to tempt us?" I said, "Because it works."

The word of God says that we are to submit to God then resist the devil. James 4:7 **Submit yourselves therefore to God. Resist the devil, and he will flee from you.** Resisting temptation without submitting to God first can be a hard row to hoe. We see this clearly with New

Year's resolutions. There is not much resolve to accomplish the resolutions because temptation enters in and reclaims its dominance in the person's life.

Jesus was tempted of the devil forty days and nights. If Jesus was tempted and he had to overcome the attraction of the temptation then what makes you think you won't have to deal with temptation? The help Jesus had is the same help and power that is available to us all who are in Christ. After Jesus was baptized, the Holy Spirit came upon Him and led Jesus into the wilderness. Luke 4:1 **And Jesus being full of the Holy Ghost returned from Jordan, and was led by the Spirit into the wilderness.**

Submission to the Holy Spirit is the answer to overcoming temptation. One of the things you will notice about Jesus is that he did not mope about because he was tempted. He overcame the temptation with the word of God. Luke 4:8 **And Jesus answered and said unto him, Get thee behind me, Satan: for it is written, Thou shalt worship the Lord thy God, and him only shalt thou serve.** After the encounter with temptation, we do not see Jesus walking around fretting over the fact that he had been tempted. Jesus immediately gets on with his life. Luke 4:14 **And Jesus returned in the power of the Spirit into Galilee: and there went out a fame of him through all the region round about.**

We also have to realize that Jesus had been fasting for forty days and nights and still had the strength to overcome sin because of the power of the Holy Spirit working within him. The blessing of our new birth with Christ is the same Holy Spirit that Jesus moved in now lives in us.

Many of us do not realize the righteous position we live in because of Christ reiging in our hearts. Becoming upset because temptation comes our way is silly. As the proverb says, **"God suffers not the soul of the righteous man to famish."** We are not some weak, just barely hanging on to a thread of God's grace saint. No, we are the blood washed Holy Spirit-filled kings and priests living in the joy of our Lord, saint. Big difference.

We are not famishing for existence and identity, wandering the spiritual edges of holiness looking for a crust of compassion. We are the sons of the most high God in Christ; benefiting from all the atoning work that was done for every man who accepts Jesus as their personal Saviour. 1John 3:1a **Behold, what manner of love the Father hath bestowed upon us, that we should be called the sons of God.**

If you are being tempted with something, then rejoice, because you are becoming a threat to the kingdom of darkness. James 1:2 **My brethren, count it all joy when ye fall into divers temptations; 3 Knowing this, that the trying of your faith works patience.** As one translation puts it: **For you know that when your faith is tested, your endurance has a chance to grow.**

Overcoming temptation strengthens our faith, and will cause the endurance of our faith to grow. Don't fear or be put out by different temptations. Overcome the tempter with the anointed power of the Holy Spirit that lives in our hearts. Amen!

SPIRIT OF MALICE

Proverbs 26:20 Where no wood is, there the fire goes out: so where there is no talebearer, the strife ceases.

George Harrison said, "Gossip is the Devil's radio."

Throw another log on the fire and see the sparks fly. It does not take much rumor to ruin a person's life. It can be a false accusation and still the damage can be irreparable even after the proof has been shown that the rumor was false. Too late, the words that were spoken start to take on a life of their own and malice is born. Out of malice comes the full maliciousness of man and all the results of that sin.

My wife has been telling me of her friend's children who have been bullied in school this year. There seems to be a new wave of it even with all the anti-bully campaigns and commercials concerning this cowardice attack. All bullying starts with hurtful words that sting and bruise the inner man. Radicalism, tribalism and selfism seem to be the polarizing factors in a lot of nations these days. Many people are just reacting to rumor and spin that is being dished out twenty-four-seven on all the McNews channels. Psalm 12:1 **Help, LORD; for the godly man ceases; for the faithful fail from among the children of men. 2 They speak vanity every one with his neighbour: with flattering lips and with a double heart do they speak.**

It has become very hard to separate truth from innuendo, or even pure malice when presented as newsworthy. Many citizens have become listless in attitude toward life as a result of drowning in all these forms of tabloid media. We end up repeating what we have heard and wonder if any of it is true, meanwhile contributing to the perpetual gossip-mill. James 3:6 **And the tongue is a fire, a world of iniquity: so is the tongue among our members, that it defiles the whole body, and sets on fire the course of nature; and it is set on fire of hell.**

The old adage, "If someone is gossiping to you, then they will gossip about you," still holds true. How do we distance ourselves from this corrosive pastime? I say corrosive because it does eventually hurt our lives in relationships and health. Prov. 26:22 **The words of a talebearer are as wounds, and they go down into the innermost parts of the belly.** What does God say we can do to overcome this attack on our human condition? James 3:2 **For in many things we offend all. If any man offend not in word, the same is a perfect man, and able also to bridle the whole body.** There it is Saints, the road to perfection is in our choices of the words we use or don't use. Having the courage to walk away from the talebearer or changing the subject is the beginning of this road to overcoming when it comes to gossip.

We read in the book of Numbers the story of Miriam and Aaron who started gossiping about their disapproval concerning Moses's foreign wife. Num. 12:1 **And Miriam and Aaron spake against Moses because of the Ethiopian woman whom he had married: for he had married an Ethiopian woman.** The result causes friction in family relations and the very health of the gossiper, Miriam. There is also another important matter that we often do not think about. God will also hear what is being said and He will step in and vindicate His anointed. Num. 12:10 **And the cloud departed from off the tabernacle; and, behold, Miriam became leprous, white as snow: and Aaron looked upon Miriam, and, behold, she was leprous. 11 And Aaron said unto Moses, Alas, my lord, I beseech thee, lay not the sin upon us, wherein we have done foolishly, and wherein we have sinned.**

As the proverb says, "The words of a talebearer are as wounds, and they go down into the innermost parts of the belly." In Miriam's case, the wound entered her skin and she had to live with that hideous condition for seven days. How was her word life after that experience? Did Miriam think twice before running off at the mouth with "Did you hear what happened to so and so?"

I say we need to think twice before entering into and giving space in our hearts to the spirit of malice. Prov. 18:21 **Death and life are in the power of the tongue: and they that love it shall eat the fruit thereof.** May blessings and good words come from our voices. Amen.

PART 1:

QUESTIONS FOR UNDERSTANDING

1. *What did you learn in this section of the book?*
2. *What surprised you the most?*
3. *What subject(s) spoke to your heart?*
4. *Did the material that you read help you understand the subject(s) more or less?*
5. *What topics are important to you? Why?*
6. *How do these articles relate to you?*
7. *After reading this section of the book, what will you change in your life?*

PART TWO:

STAY FOCUSED

Noticed, But Not Seen

Staying focused in a relationship with God can be difficult in a world with millions of distractions. However, in Christ, with an intentional choice of will, we can remain centred on the love that God has for us and focused on the purpose He created us for. Let us keep our eyes on Jesus, the author and finisher of our faith.

PHILOSOPHICAL BALONEY

Proverbs 14:16 A wise man fears and departs from evil, but a fool rages and is self-confident.

Friedrich Nietzsche stated, "They muddy the water, to make it seem deep."

Everyone has a philosophy. Even if you believe in nothing, that belief is a philosophy. I've had a few philosophical discussions over the last few weeks. Every other day I have had discussions with people who had strong and varying views of what they claimed truth was. The deeper the explanations of belief these people expounded on, the muddier the waters got. They seemed to be talking about God, but it was vague. I have heard my friend Scott say, "What is said in vagueness, stays in vagueness." 1John 4:1 **Dear friends, do not believe every spirit, but test the spirits to see if they are from God, because many false prophets have gone out into the world.**

All I could hear was a whole lot of syncretism going on. There was an amalgamation of different religions being put into the blender of supposed thoughtfulness and the mixture was coming out frothy in explanation and insipid in taste. A patchwork of cherry-picked theories to suit their own spiritual agendas was their foundational cornerstone of belief. They seemed to be making it up as they went along. Fickle interpretations did abound in speech and thought, plus they had no problem gainsaying God's clear instructions or God Himself.

One of the trains of thought was that Jesus came to teach us how to save ourselves. This implied there was no need for the blood of Jesus that takes away the sins of man, nor the need of Jesus as a personal Saviour. All we have to do is save ourselves by looking to Jesus as an example of virtue and learning to be the same through attained consciousness. Really? How can I save myself without a Saviour taking residence within my soul which is of a fallen nature and must be reborn?

How can I become born again as a new man or a new creation entirely without God setting and fulfilling the conditions of my salvation? 2Cor. 5:17 **Therefore, if anyone is in Christ, he is a new creation; the old has passed away,**

and see, the new has come! How can I do this myself, within my own godless abilities? If it were possible to save myself, then why would God have sent Jesus to the torturous cross?

Was the Crucifixion just something for pseudo-philosophers to draw examples of self-righteous tips on how to save yourself? No! The work of the cross was a serious plan the Godhead hid in Christ to save mankind from himself and eternal death! I can only be saved through Christ and not of myself. The only thing that is of my own volition is my personal choice of receiving God's gift of Jesus as my Saviour. Even within my own choice of accepting that Jesus Christ is Lord, it is still the Lord who saved me and not myself.

Another discussion that was presented as deep profoundness was that the whole Bible was only a spiritual example to draw inspiration from and not to be taken literally. I thought to myself, "Would they feel that way about the commandment 'Thou shall not murder' if they were being confronted by an axe murderer?" I am sure at that moment they would want the pragmatic reality of that biblical law to be real and honored as literal. Titus

3:9 But avoid foolish debates, genealogies, quarrels, and disputes about the law, because they are unprofitable and worthless.

We live in a world that has offered a smorgasbord of philosophical thought and has supplied the false teachers that dispense the rhetoric that goes with the said philosophy. Truth is truth. There are some who claim that there are many truths, but Jesus was the only one to say, He is the truth. Jesus did not say I will show you a way or path to truth, or there is a truth to follow, or you might like this truth if it is convenient with your belief. No saints. He said, I am the way, the truth, and the life. John 14:6 **Jesus saith unto him, I am the way, the truth, and the life: no man comes unto the Father, but by me.**

Syncretism seems to be the religious flavor of choice these days. Take the best and convenient feel-goods from different religions and make your own to suit a personal lifestyle whether God approves or not. After all, when you are saving yourself anything goes because it is personally chosen for the satisfaction of the moment. The upshot is that their foundations of truth erodes with whatever is trending at that point in history, and a syncretistic person rewrites his or her own convenient belief to act on along the way. Living in those shifting thoughts is living in absolute uncertainty and absence of God Himself, even though the word god is thrown around. Prov. 14:12 **There is a way which seems right unto a man, but the end thereof are the ways of death.** Living in this philosophical quicksand will not last.

God's grace, however, will last for an eternity. Let God save us from ourselves and our so-called intellectualism. It may not be eloquent in words by calling a belief philosophical baloney, but that is what it is. When you look up how baloney is made, you get this answer. (Usually contains afterthoughts of the meat industry - organs, trimmings, end pieces and so on.) All I can say is, "Yuck." That is what I was hearing while these people philosophized with all their afterthoughts and so on. Jesus is Lord and not an afterthought. John 15:5 **I am the vine, ye are the branches: He that abides in me, and I in him, the same brings forth much fruit: for without me ye can do nothing.**

RESOLUTIONS NEED RESOLVE

Proverbs 17:27 A man of knowledge restrains his words, and a man of understanding maintains a calm spirit.

I was reading that the average length of time a New Year's resolution is honoured and stuck with, ends around January 17th. That is it. The full ability of man within his own strength is a whole seventeen days of fortitude, gut-wrenching willpower, and bravado to accomplish a resolution that would have brought satisfaction and healthy changes to one's life. Ha! It would be funny if it were not so pathetic, but there it is. It would have been better to not have made the resolution at all because the condemnation of failure only adds to the depression the person feels and lives with already. The sense of failure is right in their face, accusing them of having no resolve to do anything.

The problem with resolutions is that the entire focus of the resolution is based on what is believed to be wrong or negative in a person's life. Lose weight, get in shape, stop eating the whole box of chocolates, stop watching so much trash television, stop polishing off the whole tub of ice cream and read more than just memes and scandal tabloids. The list is endless of what people perceive to be wrong with themselves, and it seems that is all they can focus on. Yet, there seems to be a segment of society that just gets things done the moment they set their hearts to it. I believe they have found the secret to what the Lord was saying when He said, Let your yes be yes, and let your no be no, because everything else is just frothy embellishment. Matt. 5:37 **Just say a simple, 'Yes, I will,' or 'No, I won't.' Anything beyond this is from the evil one.**

As the scripture says, all other elaboration and exaggerations beyond a plain yes or no are promoted by the evil one. In other words, talk is cheap, and Satan will help you spit out words with no intention of following up on them. Spouting off resolutions with no resolve to do them is child's play. To be determined is a choice to become disciplined. Some people say they have no motivation to be disciplined. They seem to think that people who get things done are in a constant state of motivation. This is not so, they are disciplined to do what they had been motivated for in the first place, then, they became determined to go forward. They do what is on their heart to do, rather than just talk about it. Prov. 17:27 **A man of knowledge restrains his words, and a man of understanding maintains a calm spirit.**

As I once said, when asked - what motivates you? "Motivation might help you get started, but discipline keeps you going. Discipline helps you overcome failure because failure teaches what needs to be done and what resolve has to be applied. You cannot stay continually motivated, but you can work on being continuously disciplined. Stay disciplined and motivation will inspire you to see the rewards that will come." We need the Lord's help to stay disciplined because without purpose and directions we become adrift like a ship with no rudder being tossed here and there going nowhere. Prov. 29:18a **Where there is no vision, the people perish.**

We need God's direction to do what He has sown within our hearts. Don't be afraid to ask God for the ability, strength, and fortitude to do what is in your heart. If God gives you the vision, then He will also give you the resolve and strength to accomplish the work. When we know God has sent us forth, we can also rely on His empowering grace to get the job done. Yes, there may be some great trials and tribulations, but the Lord's resolve within our hearts will wake up the courage needed for the mission. Are there possibilities of failure? Of course there is, but we will learn from the experience. As often is said, "The greatest fear is the fear of failure," and this stops people from trying. What can we ever learn if we do not learn to pick ourselves up after messing up?

We see this very thing taking place when Peter and the Apostles were threatened and commanded to stop preaching Christ. It looked like they had failed at what they were supposed to do. However, they asked God for strength to accomplish what God had put within them. Acts 4:29 **And now, Lord, consider their threats, and grant that your servants may speak your word with all boldness.** They might not have had all the answers to what God was leading them into, but there was some resolve in their character to do what God had asked them to do.

Noticed, But Not Seen

If we are going to make declarations and resolutions of faith, then let our characters be filled with the resolve to just say yes and no at the time of decision. For whatever reason we have been held back in the past, our resolution and determination for this year should be to break through into victory with the grace of the Lord leading the way. Let us be courageous with the vision God has given us. Say, "Yes Lord, with you, I can do it!" Heb. 12:1b **And let us run with endurance the race that is set before us.** Blessings.

ERRORS TO CORRECT

Proverbs 18:10 The name of the LORD is a strong tower; the righteous run to it and are protected.

Whenever one of my books is published and I receive the first copy, I look forward to reading it from cover to cover. After all, it is my work in print. However, while reading and enjoying the book, I am also looking for errors that were missed throughout the editing process. I'm not looking to discredit the process of the editors or the work itself, but rather to improve the finished work. Just because there may be a few errors, does not mean the whole book is a write-off. The mistakes that I do find are eventually corrected and the next edition of the book is a better version of itself. If an error is found, I do not throw the whole book away. I correct the mistake and look to improve as a writer. I correct the errors and go on to the next project.

Throughout life, we enact a similar editing work within our souls. With God's help, we amend what needs fixing within our lives. Through the

Holy Spirit, God corrects our errors and helps us repent of our sins. Just because we miss an instruction or mess up God's directions does not mean He writes us off and damns us to hell. The Lord forgives and heals our souls, so He can present a better version of who we are in Christ. We are never going to be more righteous than the day we accepted Christ, but we will grow in the power of His righteousness. Jesus wants to present us faultless before our Heavenly Father, and this can only be done through Christ's righteousness. Jude 1:24 **Now all glory to God, who is able to keep you from falling away and will bring you with great joy into his glorious presence without a single fault.**

The righteousness we acquired by faith in Christ does not stop us from messing up in life but guides and helps us get back on the Lord's standard of righteous living. Everything God does in our hearts is to help us become a better version of who He knows us to be. Our Heavenly Father loves us for who we are and who we will be throughout eternity. God's righteous love that He has for us is never in doubt. It protects us and keeps us from falling short of God's glory.

Prov. 18:10 **The name of the LORD is a strong tower; the righteous run to it and are protected.**

As we correct the errors of life and overcome the temptations of the enemy, we will be able to declare what the Lord says about our lives and speak faith into our future. We can express the wisdom of God because His righteous wisdom is at work within us. Prov. 16:13 **Righteous lips are the delight of a king, and he loves him who speaks what is right.** We should never forget that it is always the Lord's righteousness we are living through and not our own. This is why we do not have to panic in fright when we sin. We quickly repent and accept the forgiving grace the Lord works within us. What an amazing gift God has given us through His son Jesus.

The bible has many accounts of people who had made mistakes, sinned, and had utterly fallen. However, God had a future for them just as He has for us. Jacob tried to force God's blessing to work within his life by using his own craftiness and strength. But God demonstrated to Jacob that the blessing of the Lord could only work in God's strength. Gideon thought he was a nobody, however, the Lord revealed to Gideon who he was with God on his side. Jonathan's son Mephibosheth thought he was only a disinherited, disabled, poverty-stricken castaway, but God brought him comfort and restoration through a covenant that had been made with King David. 2Sam. 9:7 **"Don't be afraid," David said to him, "since I intend to show you kindness for the sake of your father Jonathan. I will restore to you all your grandfather Saul's fields, and you will always eat meals at my table."**

We have all sinned and fallen short of God's holy perfection. The Lord does not chuck us on the garbage heap because we messed up. He restores us and keeps leading us into better and forthright choices. There will always be mistakes, errors, and failures to overcome, but as in the example of my books, the mistakes can be corrected, fixed, and even rewritten if need be. Then, the whole rewrite can be resubmitted for publishing, thus creating a better version of what once was. Let God do the same for us. Let Him correct, guide, lead, and wash our lives through the blood of the Lord so that we come out the best version of who God says we are. Jer. 29:11 **For I know the** plans I have for you"—this is the **LORD's** declaration—"plans for your well-being, not for disaster, to give you a future and a hope. Amen and amen!

THE SHARP EDGE OF HURT

Proverbs 12:26 The righteous should choose his friends carefully, for the way of the wicked leads them astray.

You don't have to die to go to hell. Just ask long-term meth addicts how much misery, grief, and hurt they live with daily. Yes, a lot of their misery is self-inflicted, but still, their lives are a living hell and full of hurt. Ask a battered wife who is trying to escape ever-increasing brutality upon herself and her children if she thinks hell could be worse than what she is going through. There are hellholes on this earth where war is manufactured year after year, displacing families to suffer want and need. The provocateurs of these wars have no qualms sacrificing their children in the name of a just war, or as repulsive as this sounds, "A holy war." There are hurting people all over the world, and no one but God can bring relief to the sharp edge of pain these people live with daily.

We do not have to look far to realize that many people were led astray by friends and family.

We can look to our past and see how we were influenced by people who knew better but chose to hurt us anyway. Hurt people will hurt other people, so we have to create boundaries within relationships. There would not be so much pain in life if people chose their friends with care and discernment as the proverb says. Prov. 12:26 **The righteous should choose his friends carefully, for the way of the wicked leads them astray.** Many friendships are toxic, resulting in the blind leading the blind into addictions, self-harm, and mayhem, resulting in unnecessary hurts in people's lives.

It would be nice if there was a vaccine to immunize ourselves against those who are perfidious in relations, angry with life, and outright foolish in choices causing so much hurt in this world. For me, the word of the Lord is the immunizing protection that shields me from those who hurt others because of the human condition. I can walk in peace and discern the times I am living in by the leading of God's Word. Hopefully, this will also give me insight into other people's pain who are hurting all around me. God says to choose our friends carefully so that we can take care of each other and not be led astray during crazy and unstable times.

There are seven things God hates and they are listed in Proverbs 6:16-19. We who are in Christ, should not be causing strife, conflict, trouble, or discord among our brothers and sisters in the Lord. This is an abomination to our Heavenly Father because He hates this sin. Prov. 6:19 **A false witness who declares lies, and one who spreads strife among brothers.** The sharp edge of hurt is harder to get through and forgive those who caused it when the violation comes from someone in our Christian family, rather than the onslaught of hurts that come from those in the world. We expect better of those with whom we fellowship. The Psalmist was wrestling with the same emotions and pain. Psalm 55:12 **Now it is not an enemy who insults me — otherwise I could bear it; it is not a foe who rises up against me — otherwise I could hide from him. 13 But it is you, a man who is my peer, my companion and good friend!**

Jephthah was rejected by his half-brothers because Jephthah's family lineage was not perfect. Jdg. 11:1 **Jephthah the Gileadite was a valiant**

warrior, but he was the son of a prostitute, and Gilead was his father. 2 Gilead's wife bore him sons, and when they grew up, they drove Jephthah out and said to him, "You will have no inheritance in our father's family, because you are the son of another woman." Years later, when Israel was skirmishing with the Ammonites, the sons of Gilead came looking for Jephthah's help. Even though time had passed, Jephthah was still hurt by the family's rejection. Jdg. 11:7 **Jephthah replied to the elders of Gilead, "Didn't you hate me and drive me out of my father's family? Why then have you come to me now when you're in trouble?"**

There is enough hurt and pain in the world without those of us who walk in Christ causing the same problems that worldly people create through their ignorance. The unsaved population has an excuse for their actions and sinful nature, as they have not accepted the redemptive saving grace of the Lord. However, those of us who are under God's grace because we have accepted Christ as Lord should be circumspect when it comes to taking part in causing pain and suffering in a fallen world. Let us be the righteous friends that others have carefully chosen. Let us be the reason people find peace and safety in their lives. Prov. 18:24b **But there is a friend who sticks closer than a brother.** To lash out and hurt another person is easy, but to extend a hand of healing, is a divine gift from our God. Blessings.

WHAT MOTIVATES YOU?

Proverbs 25:2 It is the glory of God to conceal things, but the glory of kings is to search things out.

I have been asked many times, "What motivates you?" Well, the fact that I died for a short moment in time while having a stroke, and was prayed back to conscious life by my wife, is a major factor in what motivates me. Stepping into eternity for what seemed a long time but apparently was only milliseconds motivates me. Knowing and feeling God's pure love and presence during that infinite moment motivates me. The Lord's assignment that He has sown in my heart motivates me.

Not that I wish any harm upon anyone, but I think it would be a good experience for a lot of people to die for a moment in time and be resuscitated back to life so they can truly see how valuable their lives are. Plus, to clearly see that life is a gift from God. Deut. 30:19 **Now I call on heaven and earth to witness the choice you make. Oh, that you would choose life, so that**

you and your descendants might live! It is hard to understand the depth of life that God has given us. The Lord has literally put His eternity within us so we could be eternal beings. Eccl. 3:11 **He has made everything appropriate in its time. He has also put eternity in their hearts, but no one can discover the work God has done from beginning to end.**

You would think that God's eternal life, which is alive within us, would be enough to motivate people to want to live a full life. But, it is not that way. It seems that we have to choose life and engage with it to find its hidden secrets that keep motivating us forward throughout our time on earth. Prov. 25:2 **It is the glory of God to conceal things, but the glory of kings is to search things out.** We have to be involved in choosing life to have a meaningful purpose for our walk with God. Maybe this is why there are so many young people who are diagnosed as clinically depressed and have stopped reaching for life. They find themselves reaching for their prescriptions to give them relief from the numbness they live with all day long. They have stopped choosing life and are suffering the consequences. What motivates you to want to participate in this new day? It has to be something of eternal value and quality.

Elijah had to deal with depression and had to overcome the desire to die because of the events in his life. He was being chased by Jezebel's forces because she had sworn to destroy him. Elijah had a lot on his mind, and the pressure was getting to him. It was manifesting as a depressive death wish. 1 Kings 19:4 **Then he went on alone into the wilderness, travelling all day. He sat down under a solitary broom tree and prayed that he might die. "I have had enough, LORD," he said. "Take my life, for I am no better than my ancestors who have already died."** His defeated self-image was now blocking the truth of what God thought of him.

Only after Elijah had a genuine encounter with God and spent some quality alone time with the Lord, did Elijah get his motivation back. He was given new instructions that were in line with his calling. Elijah was to pass on the ministry mantle to Elishah. Purpose, motivation, or inspiration has to come from within our hearts as the Lord brings life to our souls and leads us into ministering His will. The reward that Elijah received for recovering from deep depression was to see the mantle of the Lord passed on to the next generation. We are all here for a limited time and we would be wise to make our time count because life truly is short. James 4:14 **Yet you do not know what your life will be like tomorrow. For you are just a vapour that appears for a little while, and then vanishes away.**

I have been fortunate to have survived a stroke and come back with good health that has allowed me to live life well. I've participated in a lot of blessed events since my recovery and have engaged in many projects God lined up for me. From writing blogs and having numerous books published to ministering and reaching people through social media platforms. These events have all been rewarding and encouraging to my spirit. However, the thing that blesses my heart the most for being here today because I responded to God's motivation, is the privilege to have seen my sons become fathers - and good fathers at that. To have seen them become great dads to their children has blessed my heart with abundant fatherly pride and joy. Prov. 17:6 **Grandchildren are the crown of the elderly, and the pride of**

children is their fathers.

What is the reward you might miss out on because you did not respond to the motivation God offered you? What motivates you? Find the answer to this question and live to its fullness. If there is nothing that comes to mind when asking this question, then ask God to reveal your purpose to you, so that you too can choose life and live. Don't wait until you are almost dead to start looking for life. Just think, if I had not been motivated to choose life. I would have missed out on that glorious moment in my life and my sons' lives. May we live long and prosper in what God has moved our hearts to do. Amen!

JESUS THE WORD

Proverbs 13:13 Whoso despises the word shall be destroyed: but he that fears the commandment shall be rewarded.

To despise means: To regard as negligible, worthless, distasteful, or to look down on with contempt.

To despise the written word of God is to despise Jesus; even if you do not like what I am saying, this is true. My late Pastor Arnold Kalamen said, "If Jesus is not Lord of all, He is not Lord at all."

The word of the Lord says that Jesus is the Word of God. John 1:1 **In the beginning was the Word, and the Word was with God, and the Word was God.** 14 **And the Word was made flesh, and dwelt among us, and we beheld his glory, the glory as of the only begotten of the Father, full of grace and truth.**

How precious is the word of God, and we have free access to its God-inspired instructions for our lives every minute and day if we want it.

This gift exists because of the sacrifice of the early believers from our own Christian history. John 4:37 **And herein is that saying true, One sows, and another reaps. 38 I sent you to reap that whereon ye bestowed no labour: other men laboured, and ye are entered into their labours.**

Our forerunners paid for the bible with their lives and today we can live in the blessing of the word of the Lord because of that sacrifice. To despise this living Word is an indictment against our responsibility and stewardship of this good news message for our times.

I heard a minister say, "God tests our faith with the prophetic word, then God tests our character with the written word. If we do not take the written word of God to heart and allow that word to cleanse and direct us forward, we will not fulfill our destiny that God has purposed for us."

Thomas Edison said, "Vision without execution is just hallucination." The Lord said it this way in James 2:20b **That faith without works is dead.** We must put our faith in the Word who is Jesus whom God gave us, because He is the only way we will get direction from

God. Heb. 1:1 **God, who at sundry times and in divers manners spake in time past unto the fathers by the prophets, 2 Hath in these last days spoken unto us by his Son, whom he hath appointed heir of all things, by whom also he made the worlds.**

After the book of Malachi was written, there are four hundred years of God's voice being silent. Man finally hears God speak again at the baptism of Jesus and His transfiguration where God says, Luke 9:35 **And there came a voice out of the cloud, saying, This is my beloved Son: hear him.** That was all God said, "Hear Him." What elaboration is needed here? Hear Him, listen to Him, believe what He says, and have faith in Him. Jesus is the Word of God and God's living Word is in us to fulfill the holy will of the Father. 1John 5:11 **And this is the record, that God hath given to us eternal life, and this life is in his Son.**

I love the Word of God and the Word loves me. 1Cor. 3:23 **And ye are Christ's; and Christ is God's.** May God's face shine on us all.

A SPIRITUAL FUNK

Proverbs 18:14 The spirit of a man will sustain his infirmity; but a wounded spirit who can bear?

Finding our way toward a Godly solution can sometimes seem hard on our human spirit. We sometimes get overwhelmed with well-meaning brothers and sisters in the Lord who try to encourage us with scriptural platitudes or scriptures like, Phil. 4:13 **I can do all things through Christ which strengthens me.** Perhaps this verse was hurled at your wounded soul. Eph. 6:10 **Finally, my brethren, be strong in the Lord, and in the power of his might.** Maybe this favorite verse was served with unquenchable enthusiasm. Ex. 14:14 **The LORD shall fight for you, and ye shall hold your peace.**

All of these sacred Scriptures are wonderful and absolutely true; however, when we are trying to overcome a battle in life, with a wounded spirit, these scriptural nuggets can make us feel like we have fallen short of some kind of qualification and all that will come out of our hearts is a question that King David asked in Psalm 43:5a **Why art thou cast down, O my soul? and why art thou disquieted within me?**

At this moment I find myself in the same position as the well-meaning brothers and sisters who want to encourage those who have been wounded to a point of personal fatalism. So I will proceed with what I feel is sensitivity toward those who have a wounded spirit.

In Timothy Keller's book, "The Reason For God," there is a story of a woman who found it very difficult in all her efforts finding God's help in her time of need. A suggestion was given to her that Christ was the great Shepherd and that she should wait to be found by Him, because she was lost and He was looking for her. Shortly afterward her testimony was, yes, Jesus had found her and she is at peace now.

This story touched me because I could look back in my life and see how true this was for me. The Lord had come looking for me on many occasions and when He found me in a fallen desperation, He loved me anyway. He cleaned me up and healed all my wounds within my spirit. Once more, He set me on His path and guided me to a loving relationship.

You might ask if I got all the answers to my questions that got me into the funk of desperation in the first place. No, I did not get all the answers because I no longer needed them. I was healed from what had been bothering me and it was time to move on as Paul says in, Phil. 3:13 **Brethren, I count not myself to have apprehended: but this one thing I do, forgetting those things which are behind, and reaching forth unto those things which are before,** 14 **I press toward the mark for the prize of the high calling of God in Christ Jesus.**

As I move forward in my Christian walk, there may be a reality check that I will not have all my goals and wishes fulfilled. However, if I stay in Christ I will be fulfilled. Is that not what everyone is looking for on this earth? Fulfilment of soul and spirit, plus the ability to be at peace with what we know about ourselves and know that we belong to our Lord.

In some people's minds, this may not be a lofty ambition, but in the eyes of God, this is a fulfilment that cannot be bought by anything we have. It has been paid for in full with the blood of Jesus, and that genuine sacrifice is a gift for us all who are wounded in spirit. We can be healed and gratified in the fullness of God's eternal love and His plan for each one of us.

So what did King David do in response to the spiritual funk he found himself in? Psalm 43:5 **Why art thou cast down, O my soul? and why art thou disquieted within me? hope in God: for I shall yet praise him, who is the health of my countenance, and my God.** For I will yet praise Him. Yes, because no matter how low we feel, where are we going to go, but Him? John 6:68 **Then Simon Peter answered him, Lord, to whom shall we go? thou hast the words of eternal life.** Amen.

Fix The Broken Walls

Proverbs 25:28 He that hath no rule over his own spirit is like a city that is broken down, and without walls.

In the years that I have walked with the Lord, I have come across many people who became casualties of their own doing. They had dug a pit and fallen into it. After talking with these hurt people, their dilemmas were a result of no longer doing what God's word said but rather they were going through the motions of hearing a religious homily. Paul said in 1Cor. 9:27 **But I keep under my body, and bring it into subjection: lest that by any means, when I have preached to others, I myself should be a castaway.**

Paul knew the danger of only talking a talk without walking through what the Lord had put in his heart to do. James 1:23 **But be ye doers of the word, and not hearers only, deceiving your own selves.** The interesting thing about not being a doer of the word of God is once you are self-deceived, the devil no longer has to spend time deceiving you because you are doing a good job of it yourself.

What was the difference between the Hebrew children and the Egyptians when the angel of death came by night? Everyone had heard the warning from Moses and Aaron. It was a clear warning to let God's people go, and if they did not, there would be death. Ex. 12:23 **For the LORD will pass through to smite the Egyptians; and when he sees the blood upon the lintel, and on the two side posts, the LORD will pass over the door, and will not suffer the destroyer to come in unto your houses to smite you.** Only those who acted on the word of God concerning using the blood of a lamb on their door frames were saved and spared great anguish. They were doers of the word, as well as hearers.

We are to be doers of the word as well as hearing what the Spirit of God is saying to do. Paul called this word, "The word of life." Phil. 2:16 **Holding forth the word of life; that I may rejoice in the day of Christ, that I have not run in vain, neither laboured in vain.** We want our lives to count for the glory of Christ because at the end of it all, we will not be saying,

"I should have spent more time at the office, or I should have built a bigger business." No, saints, we will most likely regret the fact that we did not do more in the kingdom of God by faith. Matt. 6:20 **But lay up for yourselves treasures in heaven, where neither moth nor rust doth corrupt, and where thieves do not break through nor steal.**

The word says that the devil goes around looking for someone to destroy. 1Pet. 5:8 **Be sober, be vigilant; because your adversary the devil, as a roaring lion, walks about, seeking whom he may devour.** Our enemy the devil is a liar and the father of lies. He looks for the weak and helpless in the faith to destroy them by deception. The proverb says that our walls get broken down when we no longer rule over our spirit. The word of God says in Eph. 6:17b **And take the sword of the Spirit, which is the word of God.** The word of God is the final authority in our lives and how we live it in the spirit of Christ.

The victory is ours when we rule our hearts and spirit with the guiding word of God. We are the victors and not the victims when we submit to Christ in life. Job had a hedge or wall of protection around him that frustrated the attacks of the devil, so we also can have the same comfort and protection because Jesus has already done the hard part for us. He gave His life that we could live in Him and have our being. Praise the Lord for the help of the Holy Spirit who helps us rule our spirit. Jude 1:20 **But ye, beloved, building up yourselves on your most holy faith, praying in the Holy Ghost.**

BREAKTHROUGH

Proverbs 19:8 He that gets wisdom loves his own soul: he that keeps understanding shall find good.

Have you ever seen a plant pushing through the cement causing a crack in the sidewalk? What force and determination it took (if plants have determination) for that small shoot to break through a five-inch layer of cement or pavement. This illustration can be an example of the growing power of God that is within each one of us who reach for the love and grace of our Lord to accomplish what God has put within our hearts. Luke 1:37 **For with God nothing shall be impossible.**

God admonishes us to come out from beneath the built-up debris in our lives. He has equipped us to break through that crusty layer of rubbish that has brought limitations and bondage into our relationship with our Lord. 2Cor. 6:17 **Wherefore come out from among them, and be ye separate, saith the Lord, and touch not the unclean thing; and I will receive you,** 18

And will be a Father unto you, and ye shall be my sons and daughters, saith the Lord Almighty.

With the help of the Spirit of God from within us, we can break through the heavy brass ceiling that has pushed us down to non-effectiveness within the body of Christ. The truth of Phil. 4:13 **I can do all things through Christ which strengthens me** becomes a reality when we act and believe the power of Christ working within our hearts. We can break through the heavy cement-like force of problems and temptations that are pressuring us to give up and fall down.

We sometimes think that we are so buried under sin and worldliness that God cannot find us because of the thick piles of carnality that has enveloped our beings. This is not to be believed because Jonah was in the deepest place of despair and disobedience one could imagine and yet God found him. Jonah 2:5 **The waters compassed me about, even to the soul: the depth closed me round about, the weeds were wrapped about my head. 6 I went down to the bottoms of the mountains; the earth with her bars was about me for ever: yet hast thou brought up**

my life from corruption, O LORD my God.

God does not give up on us. We tend to give up on ourselves because we forget the redeeming factor of our salvation. We can push through the hardship and sometimes demonic bondage with our trusting that Christ's redemptive work was and is complete. Rom. 5:9 **Much more then, being now justified by his blood, we shall be saved from wrath through him.** Col. 1:20 **And, having made peace through the blood of his cross, by him to reconcile all things unto himself; by him, I say, whether they be things in earth, or things in heaven.**

God knows how strong we truly are because He knows how strong He is. The Lord knows He has overcome the world and sin, and now lives within us by faith, so we have the power to break through because of what Christ has done. John 16:33 **These things I have spoken unto you, that in me ye might have peace. In the world ye shall have tribulation: but be of good cheer; I have overcome the world.**

It is no wonder God wants us to say we are strong in Him and can break through and break out because He is in us. Joel 3:10b **Let the weak**

say, I am strong. Am I oversimplifying this? Have we become so accustomed to tolerating defeat that we learn to live with it, like that squeaky cabinet drawer? The fix for the drawer is oil and adjustment, and without sounding trite, would that not be the same for us? The oil of the Holy Spirit and the adjustment of our faith in God's word toward our situation would go a long way in breaking out. Have faith in God concerning our victories. The Lord has not brought us this far in our walk with Him to drop us on a technicality of a perceived transgression invented out of our own ignorance.

No, God has done too much to secure our souls. We have to believe the love God has for us and the breakthrough will come with Christ leading the way. Jude 1:24 **Now unto him that is able to keep you from falling, and to present you faultless before the presence of his glory with exceeding joy.**

FOR TODAY TRUST THE COVENANT

Proverbs 3:5 Trust in the LORD with all thine heart; and lean not unto thine own understanding.

We often hear the statement "One day at a time." How simple a statement, but profound, since I can only be in the day I am in. I cannot go back in time nor can I go into the future. I live in the day I exist in. I cannot do anything to change the past and I cannot walk into the future until tomorrow is today. I can only take control of the day I am living in and that mandate has been given to every man on earth. Today is the day the Lord has made; therefore, what can I do for my life today that will make it worth all it can be? As I awoke this morning I made a declaration of faith for the day.

For today, God willing, I will not fear lack.

The word of God says that God will meet my needs in life. God's name is Jehovah-Jireh Gen. 22:14a **So Abraham called that place The LORD Will Provide.** The fear of not having enough is constantly being pushed on us daily. We fret over the two percent of the stuff we do not have and forget to give thanks for the ninety-eight percent of what we do have. Fretting turns to fear. Before we know it, we are worried about the future and envisioning a great disaster and being left out in the cold. No! The word of God says in Phil. 4:19 **And my God will meet all your needs according to the riches of his glory in Christ Jesus.** I will trust the covenant God has made with me. We sometimes fear our children will not be provided for. God's word says the seed of the righteous will not beg bread. Psalm 37:25 **I have been young, and now am old; yet have I not seen the righteous forsaken, nor his seed begging bread. Therefore, today I will trust the covenant God made with me.**

For today, God willing, I will not fear being left alone.

God says in His word that I am never alone and He is always with me. 1Cor. 3:16 **Don't you know that you yourselves are God's temple and that God's Spirit dwells in your midst?** As God promised in His covenant He made with all of us, He will never leave us nor forsake us. Deut.

31:6 **Be strong and courageous! Do not fear or tremble before them, for the LORD your God is the one who is going with you. He will not fail you or abandon you!** For today, I will believe God's promise and walk in the truth of it.

Just for today, I will believe God is not a man that He should lie to me. I can only live in the day I am in; therefore, taking the time during the day to realize that God is walking with me throughout the day gives me hope for today and the future. If I am at rest in the day I am in, I will be at rest when the next day comes along because it will be a new day to trust the covenant God made with me.

For today, God willing, I will not fear sickness and disease.

God's word is full of promises declaring He is a healing God and still heals today. God's name is Jehovah-Rophe. Ex. 15:26b **For I am the LORD that heals thee.** From the beginning in the Old Testament to the New Testament God's heart toward His people is forgiveness and healing. Psalm 103:3 **Who forgives all thine iniquities; who heals all thy diseases.** Fear can bring sickness and great distress in our bodies. God's first words towards us are so often "Fear not."

We have a world full of growing fear and diseases to go along with the overcharged feelings of anxiety. No wonder sickness and disease are running rampant. So many have lost the ability to just be still and be at peace for the day they are in. Psalm 46:10 **Be still, and know that I am God: I will be exalted among the heathen, I will be exalted in the earth.** For today, Lord God, I choose your peace and healing for my soul, mind and body.

For today, God willing, I will not fear what man can do to me.

Jesus said not to fear what man can do to us. Matt.10:28a **Do not be afraid of those who kill the body but cannot kill the soul.** Trusting the covenant God made with us is trusting the one who made the covenant in the first place. God is not a man that He should lie; therefore, He can be trusted. God is greater than man and because of that, I can stop fearing what man can do to me. God is truth and speaks only truth. God loves us perfectly and there is no fear in His love. 1John 4:18 **There is no fear in love. But perfect love drives out fear, because fear has**

to do with punishment. The one who fears is not made perfect in love. For today, I will trust the covenant God made with me. For today, God willing, I will not fear the fears of life. Amen!

PART TWO:

QUESTIONS FOR UNDERSTANDING

1. *What did you learn in this section of the book?*
2. *What surprised you the most?*
3. *What subject(s) spoke to your heart?*
4. *Did the material that you read help you understand the subject(s) more or less?*
5. *What topics are important to you? Why?*
6. *How do these articles relate to you?*
7. *After reading this section of the book, what will you change in your life?*

PART THREE:

A NEW SOUND

Noticed, But Not Seen

Revelation 14:2 And I heard a sound from heaven like the roar of rushing waters and like a loud peal of thunder. The sound I heard was like that of harpists playing their harps. The sound we are to listen to is the sound of the Holy Spirit, who heals our hearts, souls, and bodies to give all glory to God the Father for our eternal gift and Saviour Jesus Christ our Lord.

THE NEW SOUND

Proverbs 8:4 I call to you, to all of you! I raise my voice to all people.

Are you tired of the same old sound of "Oh hum?" Have you become a mouthpiece for all the troubles we are going through and reinforcing the magnitude of the problem by talking about it all day long? Our Heavenly Father says it is time for a new thing to be done, and a new sound to be heard. Isa. 43:19 **See, I am doing a new thing! Now it springs up; do you not perceive it? I am making a way in the wilderness and streams in the wasteland.** The wilderness experience that many are going through can be changed by obeying the direction of the Lord. If you have found yourself languishing in a desert and existing with a dry arid soul that no longer satisfies your life, then it is time for a new song to come forth from your inner man. Psalm 96:1 **Sing a new song to the LORD; let the whole earth sing to the LORD.**

What does a new sound of God sound like

or even look like? Where is the mighty wind of God that will change the negative narrative that is stagnating numerous people in the church? Acts 2:2 **And suddenly there came from heaven a sound like a mighty rushing wind, and it filled the entire house where they were sitting. 3 And divided tongues as of fire appeared to them and rested on each one of them.** The Holy Spirit is available to us, however, we have to ask for His indwelling and leading to bring about the move that God has planned for us. We have to want the sound of the Holy Spirit's visitation and revival upon our lives.

Like all revivals in the past, they have all come about because of the hunger within people's hearts for the will of God to manifest. Plus, the desire to see God moving in the earth, freeing countless souls from a Christless eternity. We all want God to move and bring about the biggest revival ever, but we have to get out of God's way so He can fulfill His will and our destiny. To simply put out an old dusty sign in front of the church saying Revival This Week, Between the Hours of 7:00 pm. to 8:30 pm. is not going to cut it. It is going to take a submissive heart toward the Holy Spirit and let Him do the eternal work within us that needs to be done to sanctify us for the Lord's use.

The new sound of the Lord is an anointed birthing of holiness that is God-inspired. God is the one who leads His people into a revival of the heart and does it in a way that all the people of the earth may take part in the outpouring of His grace. Hab. 2:14 **For the earth will be filled with the knowledge of the glory of the LORD as the waters cover the sea.** If the Lord is asking you to pray for the coming new sound of the Holy Spirit, then do not put this calling off. Prov. 8:4 **I call to you, to all of you! I raise my voice to all people.** Don't say, "God would not use me to bring about a worldwide revival because I am not that spiritually connected to Him." So many people say the same thing and this is why we need a new move of the Lord and revival in our hearts. God can and does use who He wants.

Revival is God's idea and our necessity. God does not need to be revived, we do. We want to have a sharp focus on what God is doing so that we stop approaching Sunday after Sunday with a drone-like attitude. We will die a slow death within our souls if we do not come alive to what God is up to. We were created to live and be alive in the spirit of God. To have the Lord of the universe dwelling within our hearts is not a small thing. It is beyond that which we can even imagine. The only thing stopping a renewal of the Holy Spirit's power within us is the limitations we put on God.

The new sound that will come from our hearts is a renewal of resurrection power and love for the Lord. Let us ask God what He wants to do with His church, and ask what the answer is for our lives to come into agreement with what the Lord is doing. God invites us to call upon Him for the answers we need. Jer. 33:3 **Call to me and I will answer you, and will tell you great and hidden things that you have not known.** Yes, Lord, we ask You to help us do what has to be done in our hearts, to bring about the revival that the whole world needs at this time. Father, Your will be done on earth as it is in heaven. Give us an outpouring of the Holy Spirit that we have never known or seen to this day. Let it be done. Amen!

THREE SHARP WHISTLES

Proverbs 16:20 Those who listen to instruction will prosper; those who trust the LORD will be joyful.

In the late 1950s when I was a kid playing out in the neighbourhood, all my friends, (and I mean all of my friends,) could hear my mother's loud and piercing whistles calling her kids home at day's end. As I rolled my eyes, everyone would look at me and say, "Hey Sawyer, looks like you got to go home, your mom is calling you." That was fine because it was a sign that they all had to go home too.

No saints, there were no long-lasting traumatic effects on my psyche. I know that today's sensitivities to every imaginable excuse and reason for therapy are out there. Called home by being whistled at may be detrimental and cause permanent scarring in today's child diagnosis handbook, but it was not that way back then. Being called home with the neighbourhood dogs who had also heard the high decibel whistles did not affect my charming nature or cool disposition.

I may pant and howl when a fire truck goes by, but that is no reason to diagnose me as flawed or commit me to therapy.

Those three trilling high-frequency whistles that could clearly be heard, was a direct instruction that needed no words to accompany the sounding blast. It was distinctly my mother's whistle, and it was saying, "Time to come home, and do it now!" We are the Lord's children, or as such, His kids. We also have to keep the ears of our hearts open to hearing what the Spirit of the Lord is saying and to respond when He is calling us. Whether God has a type of whistle or gentle nudge that awakens our heart when He calls, we need to know that the instruction is clear and safe to follow. John 10:27 **My sheep hear My voice, and I know them, and they follow Me.**

To hear the voice of the Lord is a tremendous blessing. Why would God make it difficult to hear His voice if He instructed us to obey His voice? Deut. 28:2 **And all these blessings shall come upon you and overtake you, because you obey the voice of the LORD your God.** Responding to God's voice should not be confusing as so many make it out to be. God's leading is clear, but on the other hand, the enemy's deceptive directions always come with condemnation and confused dysfunction. God's voice and guidance bring peace. Prov. 16:20 **Those who listen to instruction will prosper; those who trust the LORD will be joyful.**

During one of Elijah's vulnerable times in his life, he needed to hear the voice of the Lord to know what to do next. Like many people who look for monstrous signs and wonders to be led, Elijah looked for God's voice in a cyclonic windstorm that scattered rocks on a mountainside and then in an earthquake, but it was not there. After the tremors, Elijah looks in a blazing fire but the Lord's voice was not there either. It was after all the noises had settled down did he finally hear God. 1Kings 19:12b **And after the fire there was the sound of a gentle whisper.** Elijah knew that he knew he was hearing from God and he was able to proceed with the mandate of his calling.

The word of the Lord says that God speaks to us through His son Jesus. Heb. 1:2a **Has in these last days spoken to us by His Son, whom He has appointed heir of all things.**

Much confusion comes to people when they stop reading the word of God and stop inquiring of God through prayer. People forget that the word clearly says, "Jesus is the way, the truth and the life, and it is through Jesus that we will have fellowship with our heavenly Father." Keeping our ears and hearts tuned to the still soft voice or whistle God uses to get our attention is an acquired skill we are to keep learning throughout our walk with the Lord as long as we are on this earth.

As I had to learn to hear and obey the hair-raising whistle my mother used to get us home, I must keep learning and hearing the voice of the Lord that will make sure I make it to my heavenly home. Heavenly Father, your voice is a wonder to behold. Thank you, Lord, that you speak to your children clearly and precisely with love. Jude 1:24 **Now all glory to God, who is able to keep you from falling away and will bring you with great joy into his glorious presence without a single fault.** Amen and amen!

WHEN OTHERS PROSPER

Proverbs 6:34 For jealousy is the rage of a man: therefore he will not spare in the day of vengeance.

When others prosper, do you get jealous?

Years ago, my nine year old son and I were watching a TV sports report about a basketball player who had just landed a very big and lucrative contract. My son turned to me and said, "Wow, dad. Isn't that just wonderful for him getting that deal?" I had just received a lesson from God through my son. My son was rejoicing in the prosperity of others. There was no jealousy or envy in his statement, it was a genuine joy for the blessing that another person was receiving.

I heard Gloria Copeland say that we should be happy when others are being blessed because that means the blessing line is moving and your turn is coming up. Eze. 34:26 **And I will make them and the places round about my hill a blessing; and I will cause the shower to come down in his season; there shall be showers of**

blessing.

Cain would not deal with his jealousy and envy toward his brother Abel. Prov. 14:30 **A sound heart is the life of the flesh: but envy the rottenness of the bones.** The jealousy and envy within Cain caused him to strike out and kill his brother. Gen. 4:8 **And Cain talked with Abel his brother: and it came to pass, when they were in the field, that Cain rose up against Abel his brother, and slew him.**

The fact was that Cain could not rejoice in the blessing his brother was receiving from God. He would not humble himself and learn from God and his brother what was acceptable as a sacrifice to God. You might say that I am using an extreme example, but I say not at all. The news is awash in articles every day of people overreacting to jealousy, envy, and malice to the point of committing robbery and homicide.

We read in the book of Esther how Haman, because of his jealousy toward Mordecai, caused incomprehensible decisions that eventually got himself hung on a gallows because of an envy he could not deal with. Esther 3:5 **And when Haman saw that Mordecai bowed not, nor**

did him reverence, then was Haman full of wrath. Not only did his jealousy get himself killed, but he also got his ten sons killed. Esther 9:14 **And the king commanded it so to be done: and the decree was given at Shushan; and they hanged Haman's ten sons.** Talk about wreaking havoc on your family over a jealous and envious spirit.

God asks us to rejoice in the blessings of others. Deut. 26:11 **And thou shalt rejoice in every good thing which the LORD thy God hath given unto thee, and unto thine house, thou, and the Levite, and the stranger that is among you.** We are created in the image of God and He rejoices over us and knows the true peace that comes from seeing us blessed. Zeph. 3:17 **The LORD thy God in the midst of thee is mighty; he will save, he will rejoice over thee with joy; he will rest in his love, he will joy over thee with singing.**

The Lord's agenda from Genesis to Revelation is to bring us to a place of pure righteousness and blessing. He speaks blessing and prosperity over us and we, therefore, as His children should bless and rejoice in the prosperity of others because we are imitating our heavenly Father whose nature it is to rejoice in His love for us. The next time you see someone getting something you have always wanted, just say, "Isn't that wonderful" and realise the blessing line is moving and you might be next. Bless you much!

A GOOD PERCEPTION

Proverbs 31:18 She perceives that her merchandise is good: her candle goes not out by night.

One of the hallmarks of a good sales company is that they know their products are superior and will do their customers good. Their products can overcome any scrutiny and questioning that the competition can throw at it. Paul was clearly stating this when he declared in Rom. 1:16 **For I am not ashamed of the gospel of Christ: for it is the power of God unto salvation to every one that believes; to the Jew first, and also to the Greek.**

We have a superior product that can do anyone in the world good. The word of God that proclaims Christ crucified for every soul on earth has the answer to whatever ails any human being. We do not have to be ashamed or timid about our Lord Jesus, and we do not have to shy away from proclaiming Him as the answer to the human condition of lost souls. Jesus Himself said that He was the answer to all mankind. John 14:6

Jesus saith unto him, I am the way, the truth, and the life: no man comes unto the Father, but by me.

When we perceive that our Lord is the King of kings and the Lord of lords our candle will not go out by night, because Jesus is the light of the world and will shine His love on all darkness out there. We have been given this light and are encouraged to let it shine so that the world may know there is a way out of their misery. Matt. 5:16 **Let your light so shine before men, that they may see your good works, and glorify your Father which is in heaven.** No matter the need, Jesus within us can manifest any help that anyone could receive to change their lives for their eternal best.

We are the hand extended that God uses to introduce Himself to a lost world. God shows Himself as Jehovah-Jireh, our Provider. Jehovah-Rophe, our Healer. Jehovah-Nissi, our Banner. Jehovah-M'Kaddesh, our Sanctification. Jehovah-Shalom, our Peace. Jehovah-Tsidkenu, our Righteousness. Jehovah-Rohi, our Shepherd. Jehovah-Shammah, God is there. All we have to be is a willing instrument of His name. How can we not perceive living within us a Saviour of such awesome power? His thoughts of love are toward us, His creation. Psalm 139:17 **How precious also are thy thoughts unto me, O God! how great is the sum of them!**

We can also say as Paul did, we are not ashamed of the gospel of Christ because there is no other name under heaven than Jesus who can minister to all our needs in this life. Acts 4:12 **Neither is there salvation in any other: for there is none other name under heaven given among men, whereby we must be saved.**

As the proverb says, our merchandise is good and it will not expire in the dark. It will overcome any darkness and bring God-giving life to all who ask for it. John 1:12 **But as many as received him, to them gave he power to become the sons of God, even to them that believe on his name.**

FACT VERSUS TRUTH

Proverbs 22:21 To make you know what is right and true, that you may give a true answer to those who sent you?

Someone said, "God's Grace is only as visible as His truth is clear." Clearly, Jesus was and still is full of grace and truth. John 1:17 **For the law was given by Moses, but grace and truth came by Jesus Christ.** The blessing that we have in Christ enables us to discern truth and is available for us to draw upon, by faith, because the Lord of grace and truth lives and reigns in our souls.

Truth can be found, attained, and received by faith because the Lord of truth arrests our inner-man to be alert and guided by the Spirit of truth; therefore, truth is readily available when we ask for it. Phil. 4:8a **Finally, brethren, whatsoever things are true, think on these things.** Sometimes the truth can be right in front of a person and they can miss it entirely, as in the case of Pilate talking to Jesus. John 18:38a **Pilate saith unto Him, What is truth?**

Facts and truth are often perceived as interchangeable and having the same meaning; therein is the problem. This is why a self acclaimed spiritual person or immature Christian will say something like, "Well, that is your truth and this is my truth." Sorry, truth is truth and God will judge us according to our own so-called measure of truth. The plumb line that these carnal people set for themselves and others will be the plumb line God uses to show them their shortcomings. So, why not take the gift of true grace that God has provided us and that is His Son, Jesus Christ, the only way and truth to eternity with the Father. John 14:6 **Jesus saith unto him, I am the way, the truth, and the life: no man comes unto the Father, but by me.**

A cardiologist showed me the cardiogram image of the irregular heartbeat that sometimes happens to me. The doctor said, "This cardiogram shows me the truth of what is happening to you." I said, "No, this graph shows me the facts of what is happening, but the truth is, Jesus sent his word and healed me." The facts are, as the doctor says, this could cause serious problems down the road. The truth is that Jehovah-Rapha is still on the throne and wants me to be in health as my soul prospers. 3John 1:2 **Beloved, I wish above all things that thou may prosper and be in health, even as thy soul prospers.**

The facts are that a few years ago I did have a TIA (Transient Ischemic Attack). The truth is that the Lord, through the name of Jesus Christ, pulled me out of it. There are many facts going on and I value the information the dedicated doctors have given me because now I know what to pray for exactly. Phil. 4:6 **Be careful for nothing; but in every thing by prayer and supplication with thanksgiving let your requests be made known unto God.**

We can get overwhelmed by the facts in life but we are the children of the most high God and His word concerning our lives and well-being is the truth about our lives. Are there going to be hard days? Yes, absolutely, but the truth is Phil. 4:13 **I can do all things through Christ which strengthens me.** I am not being braggadocious, I am only saying what God says is the truth about my life. Matt. 9:29b **According to your faith be it unto you.**

Are doctors part of God's health plan? Yes,

they are, as many have been called to the healing ministry. However, when God's word of truth is grafted deep in our soul then it will not be long before the truth becomes the facts of our situation.

Abraham and Sarah had to believe God for ten years before Isaac the son of promise was born to them. Abraham did not consider the fact of his old age or Sarah's ability to conceive, but only considered the truth of the word God had given them. Rom. 4:19 **And being not weak in faith, he considered not his own body now dead, when he was about an hundred years old, neither yet the deadness of Sara's womb:** 20 **He staggered not at the promise of God through unbelief; but was strong in faith, giving glory to God;** 21 **And being fully persuaded that, what He had promised, He was able also to perform.** Abraham and Sarah had a lot of facts to weigh out, but the truth of God's promise won out.

Joseph was seventeen years old when he had the dreams from God. Gen. 37:5a **And Joseph dreamed a dream, and he told it his brethren; and they hated him yet the more.** The facts of his betrayal by his brothers, then the fact that he was a slave in Potiphar's house, and the fact that he was falsely accused of a crime and sent to prison were some terrible facts about his life. Thirteen years later, when Joseph is thirty years old, the truth of the dreams come true. Gen. 41:44 **And Pharaoh said unto Joseph, I am Pharaoh, and without thee shall no man lift up his hand or foot in all the land of Egypt.** Joseph was now living the truth of what God had said.

We have all been inundated with all kinds of facts that disturb our peace and life. What does God's word say about those facts that have affected our lives? Is there a better way than just being a survivor? I think there is and that is to find out by the word of God what God says about the facts we are facing and get the truth of the matter. Blessings.

THE CHURCH BODY

Proverbs 31:29 Many daughters have done virtuously, but thou excels them all.

As most of you know the Proverbs chapter thirty-one woman described from verses ten to thirty-one is a type and description of the body of Christ as in The Church. So, ladies, when some man comes quoting Proverbs thirty-one to you, you can remind him that he must act the same way because he is part of the church that Proverbs thirty-one is describing in order to bring God's grace and blessing to a lost world.

Prov. 31:29 **Many daughters have done virtuously, but thou excels them all.** This is an interesting verse. The way I see the words, "Many daughters have done virtuously" is a description of all the Lodges, Societies, Foundations, and Clubs that do great works of kindness for the world and their communities. From the Make a Wish Foundation to the Knights of Columbus, these daughters have done virtuous and very good works, but the church of the Lord excels them all.

I know I am walking in a minefield of emotional and sacred beliefs here, but nonetheless God has made it clear that His church will not be defeated by anyone's theory or hell itself. Matt. 16:18b **I will build my church; and the gates of hell shall not prevail against it.**

God has (regardless of what people think of the church) chosen to bring His word and revelation of Himself through the body of Christ, whether we like it or not. Eph. 4:11 **And he gave some, apostles; and some, prophets; and some, evangelists; and some, pastors and teachers; 12 For the perfecting of the saints, for the work of the ministry, for the edifying of the body of Christ.**

There are a lot of hurting people who were wounded in churches and, therefore, have made vows of not ever going to church again - let alone giving them their regular ten dollar offering. I am not making light of this as I heard someone say that it would be a cold day in hell if they ever give the church another ten dollars like they normally did. We need to understand that God does not need that person's ten dollars. That person needs to give the ten-spot in order to get illumination on the situation in their unforgiving heart, but that is another discussion.

The church is Christ's idea. We are the church and we, like everyone else, will bring to the location of attendance the type of church we are. There is no perfect place because everyone is being worked on by God. The Holy Spirit, is perfecting us in righteousness. John 16:8 **And when He is come, He will reprove the world of sin, and of righteousness, and of judgment.** There is a learning curve because this nurturing from God helps us get from glory to glory, and in that growth there is a struggle and the struggle might manifest as some of the things that caused us to leave the last church location.

We are basically learning to play the violin in public and often it looks and sounds bad right there in the local assembly. We end up seeing the struggles within the people who assemble in the place we call church. In the same way that we bring all our sick folk under one roof called a hospital, we bring all who are born-again and overcoming different hypocrisies under one roof called a church.

In that place we bring all the spiritual sicknesses in our lives to get healed by the great healer, Christ. That is why we give grace to each other, in Christ, because we are all dealing with something the Lord has put His finger on. Let us say God has just touched a squishy spot that causes us to show who we really are, and in that moment, hopefully, there are mature Christians around us to help us get through that particular righteous judgment from God. Gal. 6:1 **Brethren, if a man be overtaken in a fault, ye which are spiritual, restore such an one in the spirit of meekness; considering thyself, lest thou also be tempted.**

I don't know if it is possible to be part of a church without being willing to be worked on by God in public, and at the same time, be willing to be used as a hand extended of God to help the ugly in spirit and the unwashed per se. If we are looking for the Norman Rockwell picture of what we think church is or should be, then there might be a lot of church hopping going on in our lives.

We will end up right where the devil likes us to be, on the move and unstable to the point of no longer caring if we do gather with the saints. Eph. 4:27 **Neither give place to the devil.** Psalm 50:5 **Gather my saints together unto me; those that have made a covenant with me by sacrifice.** Heb. 10:24 **And let us consider one another to provoke unto love and to good works: 25 Not forsaking the assembling of ourselves together, as the manner of some is; but exhorting one another: and so much the more, as ye see the day approaching.**

We are in a place where we have to decide whether we are going to be the church that Christ wants of us to be, or continue being offended at every opportunity that comes our way. We are the body of Christ who has and will excel above all the good and valuable societies at work in the world who are bringing joy and benefits to mankind. Our mandate is to be the Lord's hand extended, introducing mankind to an eternity with our God through Christ, The Lord. Let's get on with it.

THE RICH BLESSING

Proverbs 10:22 The blessing of the LORD, it makes rich, and he adds no sorrow with it.

Solomon, in his wisdom, knew what the blessing of the Lord could do for a soul. The simple answer is the blessing of the Lord makes rich, and God adds no sorrow with His blessing. The incredible thing about the blessing of the Lord is that it brought no harm in itself to the one being blessed. James 1:17 **Every good gift and every perfect gift is from above, and comes down from the Father of lights, with whom is no variableness, neither shadow of turning.**

It is a pure blessing, but the person who has the blessing bestowed upon their life could end up abusing it and causing the blessing to become a burden in life. When God hands us a blessing, it comes to us full and pure, but when we start thinking that we are above the law per se we can end up desperately wanting and the blessing becomes too hot to handle. We are the ones who end up turning the blessing into sorrow.

We read in God's word some of the people who could not or would not give reverence to the blessing that had been given to them. Eli, who had the blessing of priesthood on himself and his sons, lived to see the blessing of the Lord turn into sorrow. 1Sam. 4:11 **And the ark of God was taken; and the two sons of Eli, Hophni and Phinehas, were slain.**

King Saul was anointed with the blessing of being king, but Saul turned this blessing into sorrow through his arrogance and fear. 1Sam. 16:1a **And the LORD said unto Samuel, How long wilt thou mourn for Saul, seeing I have rejected him from reigning over Israel?**

Ananias and Sapphira were blessed with property and wealth. The possessions that were a blessing of the Lord, over time possessed Ananias and Sapphira, ending up a great sorrow and loss of life. Acts 5:3 **But Peter said, Ananias, why hath Satan filled thine heart to lie to the Holy Ghost, and to keep back part of the price of the land?**

In our own time and church history, we have seen the same thing with some unfortunate TV Evangelists who suffered great sorrow when they mistook the blessing of the Lord as some personal lawless license to live without regard for the heart of God. There seems to be a running theme among all these examples. There is a lack of reverence for the blessing itself and a sense of entitlement or a stout heart that says, "It's about time this blessing happened, I've been believing for it to come in and not too soon at that."

Let's look a bit deeper than just material blessing. The blessing of the LORD, it makes rich, and He adds no sorrow with it. God wants us in a receptive position of His blessing so we can be God's people and He would be our God. Jer. 24:7 **And I will give them an heart to know me, that I am the LORD: and they shall be my people, and I will be their God: for they shall return unto me with their whole heart.** That is the blessing of the Lord. Psalm 133:3b **For there the LORD commanded the blessing, even life for evermore.**

The blessing of the Lord is an amazing gift because it puts us right in the center of His love. If we could think outside the box of our limited stuff-owning-lifestyles and direct our hearts to what is the true blessing of the Lord, we would see how rich we really are in the saving grace of our God. Rom. 4:6 **Even as David also describes the blessedness of the man, unto whom God imputes righteousness without works, 7 Saying, Blessed are they whose iniquities are forgiven, and whose sins are covered. 8 Blessed is the man to whom the Lord will not impute sin.**

When we start seeing the priceless value of our salvation and bless the Lord for the way He has taken all sorrows from our hearts, we will begin to see how rich and blessed we truly are. Happy is the man whose sins are forgiven, happy is that man. 1Cor. 6:20 **For ye are bought with a price: therefore glorify God in your body, and in your spirit, which are God's.**

NADSAT: LANGUAGE OF VIOLENCE

Proverbs 4:16 For they cannot rest until they do evil; they are robbed of sleep till they make someone stumble.

In 1971 when I was eighteen years old, the ultra crime movie for its day, *Clockwork Orange*, hit the movie theatres. The publicity promoting the film inferred that the 'Ultraviolence' ideology expressed in the film may become a reality in our future. The idea that gangs or mobs of sociopaths going out on a Saturday night just to beat up the homeless, rape the helpless, and torture the mentally ill while communicating in a language of violence, or Nadsat as it was called, was to my friends and I, definitely a work of fiction. We had never thought that this scenario could become a reality in our lifetime.

Well, we were totally wrong. Nadsat is becoming the language of so many angry people these days. A coded lingo of violent expression punctuated with actions of cruelty upon ordinary citizens is now a reality. Matt. 24:12 **And because**

lawlessness will be increased, the love of many will grow cold. It is no longer unusual to come across an obnoxious bully picking on and screaming at a nurse, waitress, store clerk, or stewardess who has simply shown up for work, but now, having to physically defend themselves against the viciousness of these ignorant blackguards.

This loud tumultuous castigating against people should not be the expression of anyone in the church. However, Nadsat or violent language is slipping into some Christian's vocabulary and attitudes. If this is becoming the way of the church, then what relevance is the church if we are no different than any street gang? The word of the Lord instructs us to have grace in our language towards all people, and not words of toxicity that blow people over. Col. 4:6 **Let your speech always be gracious, seasoned with salt, so that you may know how you should answer each person.** The word says, let our speech always be gracious. Is cursing at our nurses and service workers gracious? Is shoving a store clerk to the floor and belittling them God-inspired? Is this how God treats us?

There is a vacuum of righteous leadership in the world. Because of this vacuum, the fears within the people of the world are culminating into a global vicious language of darkness that is collectively growing in the hearts of man. As this darkness takes root on a world scale, it is manifested through these evil expressions of hate. The caustic eruptions toward vulnerable employees and the man on the street are the fruit of fear and perceived helplessness so many disenfranchised people are living with. Therefore, ignorance moves these souls to express anger at everything and everyone. Prov. 4:16 **For they cannot rest until they do evil; they are robbed of sleep till they make someone stumble.** The hopelessness they are living in is palpable and raw in their hearts and they do not know how to react. So, acting out of a child's tantrum, they lash out.

As Christians, what are we becoming if our first reaction is to express angry hate? This Hatred-Virus that is spreading within mankind is more dangerous than any disease. The language of violence toward any form of authority seems to come so easily out of the mouths of those who were once in control of their emotions.

What infectious virus has entered the hearts of once reasonable people who professed to be Christians? 2Tim. 3:5 **They will act religious, but they will reject the power that could make them godly. Stay away from people like that!**

Supporting the idea of harming and belittling people is not what God called us to do. Our Lord has asked us to be His hand extended that would reach out and bring peace to those who are anguishing in their souls. We are to comfort the nurse who has been cursed at for simply going to work to take care of the sick. We are to help the store clerk off the floor who was knocked down for doing what his manager asked him to do. We who are in Christ have the message of peace and love the world is so desperate to hear. Mark 16:15 **Then he said to them, "Go into all the world and preach the gospel to all creation.**

The Gospel is the good news and not a violent language of hate. The word of the Lord sets us free from bondage. God's word does not let us participate in the rhetoric of simpletons who are agitating the crowds to vocalize their pustulant edicts of nonsense. There is nothing wrong with participating in peaceful protests to point out unrighteousness and harmful laws that truly hurt a society. However, let us do it with the scriptural basis that gives us the honest conviction of heart to be out there. While marching and speaking up for those who cannot speak for themselves, let us speak with God's language of grace which is salted with His love.

Before you lash out in the language of Nadsat remember that God so loved the world that He gave us Jesus. The punishment that so many people feel someone else deserves was placed upon Jesus so that we would have eternal life and peace. May God's face shine on you and give you the desires of your heart according to His will. Love you much.

STOP THE WAR

Proverbs 20:18 Every purpose is established by counsel: and with good advice make war.

The red placard was big and bright with the words "Stop The War." I thought to myself, "Which war? There are so many."

The world is awash in wars, skirmishes, battles and conflicts. There are so many types of wars that the buzz word in some cases when land, sea, and air battles are involved, it is called, "theatre of war." There is a war on drugs, gangs, terrorism, borders, waterways, ideologies, and a war for the souls of mankind. Wars will not be stopped until the warring within our souls is stopped, controlled or repented of.

Until there is an honest desire within our hearts for the success of our neighbours, workmates or men on the street - wars will not stop. When a territory or a radical religious idea is being fought over to the point of a full-blown war, then wars and conflicts will remain in full explosion until everyone is dead, or the sickening waste of it all is finally seen for what it is.

The word of God says that wars are going on because the war within our hearts is causing conflict. James 4:1 **What causes conflicts and quarrels among you? Don't they come from the passions at war within you?** This conflict is the result of the fallen human condition. As long as there are humans on the earth, war will be an option.

The battle within our souls is to be conquered and eventually to have victory over what it is that causes the unrest. These clashes within us will be defeated when we allow the power of the Holy Spirit to become the peacemaker in our lives. 2Cor. 10:3 **For though we walk in the flesh, we do not war after the flesh: 4 For the weapons of our warfare are not carnal, but mighty through God to the pulling down of strong holds.**

Most people at war do not realize that they are fighting against an enemy that is trying to defeat, destroy and eradicate the human race. The word of God is clear that we are battling princely powers, demon influences and not humanity. Eph. 6:12 **For we wrestle not against flesh**

and blood, but against principalities, against powers, against the rulers of the darkness of this world, against spiritual wickedness in high places. If we want to stop endless wars, then we will have to stop the enemy of our soul who has been promoting his own type of evil crusade through racism, bigotry, poverty, sickness and disease. When we become the neighbours we want to have, then we will begin to stop the war.

The elimination of war starts with the full capitulation of our own souls to the Lord Jesus. Someone has to surrender first. Christ surrendered to the cross so that we could surrender to Him and be victorious in a resurrection life as Jesus is. 1John 4:17 **Herein is our love made perfect, that we may have boldness in the day of judgment: because as he is, so are we in this world.** By surrendering to Christ the King of kings and the Lord of lords who conquered the cause of war by His blood which was spilled on the cross for us all, we can be assured of a true and honest victory because we are one with and in Christ. As we choose peace, war will diminish. As we choose life, abortion, murder and hatred will be seen for what it is. When we choose the solution to any problem, then the result will be a positive change of righteousness. Deut. 30:19 **This day I call the heavens and the earth as witnesses against you that I have set before you life and death, blessings and curses. Now choose life, so that you and your children may live.**

Making God-like choices on a daily basis will bring about better results than just being against everything. When we put our energies into using the wisdom, guidance and spiritual common sense God gave us, then it will bring about whole and real solutions. We will have a forward looking vision rather than the feeling that empty rhetoric is falling on deaf ears. Prov. 3:5 **Trust in the LORD with all your heart and lean not on your own understanding; 6 in all your ways submit to him, and he will make your paths straight.**

As the Proverb says, "With good advice make war." We are to fight the good fight of faith and with the Holy Spirit as our counselor directing our battle plan, we will win the war set before us because Jesus has overcome the world. John 16:33 **I have told you these things, so that in**

**me you may have peace. In this world you will
have trouble. But take heart! I have overcome
the world.**

So, what can I do to stop the war? I must
start with my own heart by extinguishing the war
within myself by allowing the righteousness of
Christ to have complete ownership of my soul.
If that is what it takes, then so be it. Lord Jesus,
I surrender all!

YOU'RE ONE OF A KIND

Proverbs 8:27 When He prepared the heavens, I was there: when he set a compass upon the face of the depth.

Why did God make my nose this way? Well, you're one of a kind. Why did God make me so short? Because you're one of a kind. Why did God make me this color? Must I say it again, "You're one of a kind!" You are a God-thought. He thought of you and here you are in full splendor of your uniqueness. Psalm 139:13 **For you created my inmost being; you knit me together in my mother's womb.**

Even your doppelganger might look just like you, but they are without controversy one of a kind; just as you are. We are absolutely irreplaceable; that is how unique we are. Once you are gone from this earth so will your uniqueness be gone. The only thing left that will be you will be what was sown in others. That's what will remain here, only what was sown. Hopefully, it will still be encouraging others to go forth and fight the good fight of faith.

Everyone has something to offer the kingdom of God and can be a blessing in this world. You don't have to do anything magnanimous or earth-shattering for God to notice your uniqueness and abilities. After all, He did give you all your attributes. Unlike the tabloid lives of the rich and shameless whose whole persona and dedication in life is to get noticed by someone for personal validation, we have already been noticed by the Lord God Himself. Jer. 1:5a **Before I formed you in the womb I knew you, before you were born I set you apart.**

Have you ever noticed when sitting down to a big family meal how everyone is so different and has various likes and dislikes? Lots of pronouncements of yum and oh, that looks good. There are even a few silent yuks that are expressed, "None for me, thank you." Some of the family members show up at the table dressed and courteous and others look like they are in permanent dress-down Fridays with the manners of a - well, you know what I mean.

All these differences are what makes us one of a kind. We truly are unique individuals, uncommon, and even extraordinary. With those differences we are to stir up ourselves toward the blessing of God's calling with what God has put in each one of us. 2Tim. 1:6 **Therefore I remind you to stir up the gift of God which is in you through the laying on of my hands. 7 For God has not given us a spirit of fear, but of power and of love and of a sound mind.**

Look at the different apostles Jesus had in His company. From a traitor, Judas, to the warm and loving heart of John who took care of Jesus' mother after His crucifixion and resurrection. Jesus also had compulsive Peter who thought nothing of cutting off the ear of a priest's servant. John 18:10 **Then Simon Peter, who had a sword, drew it and struck the high priest's servant, cutting off his right ear. (The servant's name was Malchus.)**

The Lord, through the Holy Spirit, hand picked Thomas who wanted the reassurance of the resurrection power of God. When Thomas had it, he went on to evangelize and preach the Gospel outside the Roman empire as far as India. What a unique band of brothers these men were. Truly, all of these men were one of a kind and because of their uncommon valor we reap the benefits of their work sown even though they are no longer on earth.

Give praise to God for your unique selves. Rev. 4:11 **You are worthy, our Lord and God, to receive glory and honor and power, for You created all things; by Your will they exist, and came to be.** When was the last time you thanked God for your personal creation in His image and was grateful for it? No one but you can thank God the way you do because you're truly one of a kind. No one says praise the Lord the way you say it. Your voice print and fingerprint plus your way of looking at life through God's eyes are only yours and your God's.

When Christ is your Saviour there is absolutely no one in the universe like you. When God was covenanting with Abraham about his descendants, God says something so wonderful. Gen. 15:5 **He took him outside and said, "Look up at the sky and count the stars--if indeed you can count them." Then he said to him, "So shall your offspring be."** Wow! Not one star in the universe is like another and therefore not one person in history or life is like another.

We truly and most assuredly are one of a kind. Prov. 8:27a **When He prepared the heavens, I was there.** I was there in God's thoughts and for that personal love and grace God has given me, I shout, "Praise the Lord." Most certainly you can do the same. Yes, "PRAISE THE LORD," we shout, for each one of us is one of a kind! Amen and amen!

PART THREE:

QUESTIONS FOR UNDERSTANDING

1. What did you learn in this section of the book?

2. What surprised you the most?

3. What subject(s) spoke to your heart?

4. Did the material that you read help you understand he subject(s) more or less?

5. What topics are important to you? Why?

6. How do these articles relate to you?

7. After reading this section of the book, what

will you change in your life?

PART FOUR:

THINK ABOUT IT

Noticed, But Not Seen

God says, "Come and let us reason together." Come and think things through with God. What an amazing love God has for us that He invites us to search out the mysteries of our life through His son Jesus, and lean on His creative hand that is extended towards us.

WHY CAN'T I HEAR GOD?

Proverbs 29:1 He who is often reproved, yet stiffens his neck, will suddenly be broken beyond healing.

The hardest question to answer while in a counselling session is when someone says, "Why can't I hear God? If I could hear Him audibly, then I would do what He says, and I would not be so confused." This is a common statement and assumption that is often made. This will be hard for some to accept but, why would God speak audibly to you when you have not obeyed His written word? His word says - not to gossip, and yet, you are gossiping, what difference would an audible voice make saying the very same thing? Most people write off their inner voice or internal monologue as white noise. If we cannot obey the written word which God has laid out in the Bible, we will not obey the voice from heaven, regardless of how loud it is. We will get caught up in the awe of the experience for a while, but this does not mean obedience is automatic.

As the counselling progresses and with a few probing questions, it is not long before the truth of the matter is laid out before us. There are all kinds of instructions in God's word that the person needing counselling has been ignoring habitually. They have not been faithful in the little things, therefore they cannot get much out of their Christian walk. They seem to stay in a state of stagnation with no joy. Luke 16:10 **If you are faithful in little things, you will be faithful in large ones. But if you are dishonest in little things, you won't be honest with greater responsibilities.** I realize this observation may be too simple a diagnosis, but it is on track. Our conscience is one of the methods God uses to get through to us, and if we are not following the conviction of heart pulsating within our soul and mind, hearing an audible command will become just as easy to put aside.

There can be confusion when the audible voice is thought to be heard. When Jesus cried out from the cross "Eli, Eli, lama sabachthani?" That is to say, "My God, my God, why hast thou forsaken me?" What Jesus said and what the crowd heard were two different things. Matt. 27:47 **And some** of the bystanders, hearing it, said, "This man is calling Elijah. The carnal man does not hear the heart of the Spirit. In some cases, this is what happens when the audible voice of God is heard or perceived to be heard. It becomes a discussion of what was thought to be said, thus missing the point of what was said. This is why the Lord speaks to us through the Holy Spirit and the still small voice within our hearts. We hear the intimate love language the Lord woos us with.

When Peter, James, and John were with the Lord on the mount of transfiguration, the audible voice of God the Father was heard. Matt. 17:5 **While Peter was still speaking, a bright cloud enveloped them, and a voice from the cloud said, "This is My beloved Son, in whom I am well pleased. Listen to Him!** The audible voice of God had no long-lasting effect on Peter as he ended up denying he even knew Christ at the Lord's arrest and false trial. James had scattered with the other apostles. There was no extra-human strength because they had heard God's audible voice. The only thing that brought them all back to a form of unity in Christ was the word that had been sown in their hearts. Luke 24:32

They said to each other, "Did not our hearts burn within us while he talked to us on the road, while he opened to us the Scriptures?

What God has given to those who are in Christ, is intuitive knowledge of what is said through the word to their hearts. Interestingly, it is Peter who makes the point, - we have all that we need and can be confident in the Holy Spirit to hear God through His word. 2Pet. 1:19 **We have even greater confidence in the message proclaimed by the prophets. You must pay close attention to what they wrote, for their words are like a lamp shining in a dark place—until the Day dawns, and Christ the Morning Star shines in your hearts.**

The instructions that come from God can always be found in His word. We want the verification of what God is saying in our hearts to be confirmed in His word because the competing voices for our soul will gladly tell us anything we want to hear. 1Pet. 5:8 **Be sober-minded; be watchful. Your adversary the devil prowls around like a roaring lion, seeking someone to devour.** If you are having a hard time hearing God, then take stock of what your discomfort is telling you within your conscience. Most of the time when we cannot hear God for the noise in our lives, it is because the Lord has already told us what is what, and we want another answer other than the one we got.

I agree that every once in a while there will be a clear and precise audible directive from the Lord that makes knowing what to do perfectly understandable. However, when this happens, it is because you were seeking God with all of your heart with no conditions attached. You were completely surrendered to whatever God asked of you. Jer. 29:13 **And ye shall seek me, and find me, when ye shall search for me with all your heart.** In most cases, the audible voice you heard came from your spirit and impacted you to the point that you could have sworn it was so loud that everyone around you heard it as well. Still, at this point, God's word will confirm what the Lord is saying to your soul.

We can trust the word of the Lord, and through prayer, allow the Holy Spirit to direct our lives with peace within our conscience. 2Tim.3:16 **All Scripture is inspired by God and is profitable for teaching, for rebuking, for correcting,**

for training in righteousness, 17 so that the man of God may be complete, equipped for every good work. We can hear God when we are honestly receptive and are willing to do His will. May God's face shine on us all.

BY HIMSELF

Proverbs 14:26 In the fear of the LORD there is strong confidence, and His children will have a place of refuge.

As a grandparent, it is fun to hear our children point out all the things the grandbabies did, 'all by themselves.' With wonder and exuberant voices, the description of the antics and monumental feats the babies have accomplished in their very short time from birth is awe-inspiring. We are told with a wide-eyed wonderment that the child is climbing out of the crib once the lights are out, scaling the bookshelf, and emptying the cabinets of all the pots and pans during the crawling stage. These grandiose achievements are reported and documented like the biggest world events going on in our time. "She did it, all by herself, and he did it, all by himself," is the admiration being expressed. And why not be excited, they are our prodigy. Psalm 127:3 **Children are a gift from the LORD; they are a reward from him.**

Our Heavenly Father says the same thing when it comes to the finished work of the cross where Jesus gave His life. There is total agreement from God the Father and the Holy Spirit, saying that Jesus Christ by Himself saved mankind with His own precious blood. Heb. 1:3b **When he had by Himself purged our sins, sat down on the right hand of the Majesty on high.** There is nothing we can do to enhance the work Christ accomplished through His sacrifice. It was God's idea, and through the power of the Holy Spirit, Jesus saved our souls. The Godhead put their perfect salvation plan together and there is nothing we can add to it. All we can do is accept this amazing grace-filled gift of our Lord's salvation. Eph. 2:8 **For by grace you have been saved through faith, and that not of yourselves; it is the gift of God.**

All by Himself, Jesus Christ put His life on the cross, that we could have an eternal relationship with our Heavenly Father. Throughout the scriptures, God makes it very clear that mankind cannot do anything in himself to measure up to God's standard of holiness. No amount of manmade works or sacrificial output could meet the requirements of an acceptable sacrifice to take away the sins of mankind. God has always said to look to Him and no other for salvation. Isa. 45:22 **Look to Me, and be saved, all you ends of the earth! For I am God, and there is no other.**

Charles Spurgeon had a wonderful understanding of our Lord's grace and salvation. His simple statement of "Look to Christ and live," says it all. His realization of (not by works are you saved) was made clear to Charles. He expressed that all we could do from our fallen state was - look to Jesus. Everything else was mankind's mangled attempt at working for salvation. I just love the simplicity of this insight. Look to Christ and live, is all I can do to be accepted by The Mighty God of all creation. Wow! No wonder Jesus said, Matt. 11:28 **Come to Me, all you who labor and are heavy laden, and I will give you rest.** Jesus knew what heaviness man was carrying within his soul. The need to be accepted by God but not knowing how to get there.

Jesus could see all the human effort that was going into trying to save themselves had become a tiresome, laborious burden in life because

God's requirements could not be met or even found. Salvation was a mystery hidden in Christ. Therefore, the Lord's statement "I am the way, and the truth, and the life," must have been a refreshing balm within the souls of all who truly heard Him. A confident awakening would have been realized because the words Jesus was using had life. Prov. 14:26 **In the fear of the LORD there is strong confidence, and His children will have a place of refuge.**

By Himself, Jesus endured the punishment and shame of the cross so that I would not have to go there. By looking to Jesus, I became crucified with Him. The Lord's work is my eternal reward. Gal. 2:20 **I have been crucified with Christ and I no longer live, but Christ lives in me. The life I now live in the body, I live by faith in the Son of God, who loved me and gave himself for me.** Yes, in a similar way that we smile at our children's accomplishments, our Heavenly Father smiles at His son Jesus, because by Himself, He secured our eternal inheritance. Thank you, Jesus, that we can lay down our striving and burdens at your scarred feet. What a wonderful saviour we have. Amen!

NOTHING TO LOSE

Proverbs 25:28 A person without self-control is like a city with broken-down walls.

When a person reaches the bell curve of their struggle, this is when that person has to dig the deepest within their soul to break through and overcome the unwanted addiction, bad-habit, or toxic codependent relationship that has to be broken. You may even hear someone say at this point, "You have nothing to lose but your chains, so keep fighting." Thank God the Lord is there to help us conquer the vice the enemy has tried to destroy us with. 1Chron. 14:11 **So David and his troops went up to Baal-perazim and defeated the Philistines there. "God did it!" David exclaimed. "He used me to burst through my enemies like a raging flood!" So they named that place Baal-perazim (which means "the Lord who bursts through").**

How did we get to a place in our life where we were left so vulnerable to the attack of the devil that even an addiction took over our will?

In most cases, self-control was no longer being practiced in our everyday choices. Prov. 25:28 **A person without self-control is like a city with broken-down walls.** Our walls of defence were breached because we became careless with our words, choices, and attitudes. The Lord has placed a wall of protection around us but we have to maintain the integrity of that wall as we walk with our Lord and live in our salvation. Job 1:10a **You have always put a wall of protection around him and his home and his property.**

If you find yourself in a place of utter desperation because of the mess you created within your own life, please be assured there is a way out. If you are at the bottom of an endless grave and the shadows of death are stalking your every move and thought, please know there is a mighty God who can deliver you. You have nothing to lose but the chains that have you bound at this time. Christ is well able to turn your life around and break every chain that has been wrapped around your life squeezing your very essence away. Psalm 107:14 **He led them from the darkness and deepest gloom; He snapped their chains.**

The madman of Gadara had nothing to lose but the insanity the devil was destroying him with and the chains the villagers had bound him with. Mark 5:5 **Day and night he wandered among the burial caves and in the hills, howling and cutting himself with sharp stones. 6 When he saw Jesus from a distance, he ran and fell on his knees in front of him.** It is amazing that this man did not start in with all the false humility like "How can Jesus love a demon-possessed guy like me? Or, how can God ever forgive a super sinner like I am?" and all the rest of that self-righteous rubbish people come up with in the middle of their despair.

In the full-blown manifestation of blasphemous howling, self-harm, and demon-driven insanity, the possessed man saw Jesus and ran to Him and worshiped. The madman had nothing to lose but what he had become to this point in his life. No matter the mess you are in, Jesus our Lord came to save sinners and that includes you and me. We have nothing to lose but the filth and detritus we have created in our lives. If we hand our lives over to the Lord and let Him exchange our sin-stained souls for

His salvation, we will be victorious in Christ. Isa. 61:3 **And provide for those who grieve in Zion—to bestow on them a crown of beauty instead of ashes, the oil of joy instead of mourning, and a garment of praise instead of a spirit of despair. They will be called oaks of righteousness, a planting of the LORD for the display of his splendor.**

There is nothing in this world that will be coming with us when we die. We really have nothing to lose but our souls. Since this is the reality, our life's efforts should be, to live fully with the gift God has given us through Christ. As we have so often heard from the scriptures, "For what shall it profit a man, if he shall gain the whole world, and lose his own soul?" This question has to be answered. We have nothing to lose on this side of eternity and so much to gain as we enter eternal life with all that God has for us. What an amazing gift salvation is for those who choose it. Blessings.

Norm Sawyer

DANGEROUS FOOLS

Proverbs 17:12 Better to meet a bear robbed of her cubs than a fool bent on folly.

It is a long list, but these are a few synonyms for the word fool - idiot, halfwit, blockhead, buffoon and dunce to name a few. Well, saints, according to the above proverb, it is better, and in some translations, safer to meet a bear robbed of her cubs than to hang out, work with, or be married to a fool. I live in the province of British Columbia where bear encounters are common. The result can turn out very gruesome for anyone who has been chased, attacked, or mauled by a bear.

On one hot summer day, I had to pull over on the side of the highway at the top of the Kootenay Pass. It is common for car engines in hot weather to overheat as cars progress up the precipitous thirty-kilometre uphill grade to the summit. As I was waiting for the car engine to cool down a bit, two bear cubs came ambling out of the side forest crossing the road right in front of my car.

The hair on the back of my neck started to point heavenward as I looked all around for the mother bear. It was not a secure or comfortable feeling to know that I might be in between a protective she-bear and her cubs. As far as I was concerned, the car engine had cooled down enough, it was time to go.

It is unsettling to see the brute strength, agility, and speed that a bear can use to attack. The instinctive fierce clawing used to lash out can result in someone's permanent scarring and even death. Yet, God's word says that I am better off confronting a mother bear in her instinctive protectiveness than a fool who is bent on carrying out his foolishness. It seems that fools are more dangerous than a bear coming toward us with menacing intentions and territorial bravado. Prov. 17:12 **Better to meet a bear robbed of her cubs than a fool bent on folly.** It really makes one think about the hidden dangers that hanging around a fool can cause in one's life.

On numerous occasions, I have counselled people to get rid of the fools, losers, and narcissists in their lives. For some reason, people think they can instruct a fool, and the fool will take the advice and change their life. The word clearly says that foolishness cannot be beaten, ground, or pulverized out of these people. Prov. 27:22 **Though you pound the fool in a mortar with a pestle along with crushed grain, his foolishness still will not leave him.** This is a heart issue, and only God can fix a heart. A fool bent on foolishness is dangerous because the foolish sins they get involved with have an eternal effect and can bring damage to everyone involved with them.

In 1Samuel chapter twenty-five there is a story of a foolish man named Nabal who was bent on being irresponsible in his decisions, regardless of the fact that his decisions would bring death to him and possibly his family. His wife's name was Abigail, and she was an intelligent and forthright woman. Nabal's name actually means **fool**, or, **folly is with him.** It did not matter that Nabal was married to a wise, influential, and courageous woman, he still remained stupid and made choices accordingly. The situation begs the question, how did Abigail end up married to such an idiot. I'm guessing that it was most likely an arranged marriage as was common in that day.

Nonetheless, her wise and fast actions saved her people and servants whom David was on his way to destroy because of the foolish way Nabal had treated David's men.

In this case, it truly was better for Nabal's family and staff to meet a bear robbed of her cubs than the swords of destruction that were coming down upon all of them. Abigail's courage over folly saved the day. 1Sam. 25:32 **David said to Abigail, "Praise be to the LORD, the God of Israel, who has sent you today to meet me. 33 Thank God for your good sense! Bless you for keeping me from murder and from carrying out vengeance with my own hands.** Within ten days of this event, Nabal died of heart failure and remained a stupid man till the end. The account of his life is a demonstration of foolishness. Surely we can choose better.

We live in a time when foolishness is praised and even rewarded. Sin is bragged about and flaunted on all forms of visual media platforms. Just because many people are living this way does not mean we have to be stupid too. God has given us the choice to choose His righteousness through Christ so that we are not counted among the dangerous fools who have chosen their own worldliness. To walk with God is to walk in wisdom. To walk with God is to receive understanding in our hearts. Prov. 9:10 **The fear of the LORD is the beginning of wisdom, and knowledge of the Holy One is understanding.** Let us keep clear of dangerous bears and fools alike, and allow God to instruct our hearts in choosing His life-giving wisdom. Amen!

GOOD OR BAD

Proverbs 11:27 He that diligently seeks good procures favour: but he that seeks mischief, it shall come unto him.

Why do bad things happen to good people? Why do good things happen to bad people? These are the questions that baffle philosophers and theologians alike. Matt. 5:45 **That ye may be the children of your Father which is in heaven: for he makes his sun to rise on the evil and on the good, and sends rain on the just and on the unjust.**

What we are calling bad in the moment might be the very vehicle that will drive us to the promised land. I will not get on the book of Job soapbox today. I would rather look at Noah who had to work hard labor for years to build an ark of deliverance because of the evil of others. When God closed the door of that ark, Noah and his family might have felt that the arduous years of preparation were finally a good thing.

When Joseph emerged from the pit of the

prison and overnight became the second in command in Egypt, he might have thought, "Praise God that was then and this is now." You will notice that when it has been raining for five or six days in a row, the moment the sun comes out it no longer seems to matter that the weather had been poor. The fact remains that the weather is now lovely. Likewise, are many of the tests that we go through to work out our faith in Christ. Phil. 2:12 **Wherefore, my beloved, as ye have always obeyed, not as in my presence only, but now much more in my absence, work out your own salvation with fear and trembling.**

When Ruth's husband and brother-in-law died, the times were hard emotionally and economically. She had chosen to take care of her mother-in-law and was working where she could in order to find food. When the favour of God came to her by the way of a kinsman redeemer named Boaz, the events and bad memories of the past began to fade. That was then and now Ruth was on her way to becoming King David's great grandmother. Ruth 4:13 **So Boaz took Ruth, and she was his wife: and when he went in unto her, the LORD gave her conception, and she**

bare a son. This possibility for Ruth's life looked bad, back in Moab, but God turned it all around.

When the first Christians of the faith were being persecuted and murdered by Saul of Tarsus, it looked grim for the first saints. Acts 7:58 **And cast him out of the city, and stoned him: and the witnesses laid down their clothes at a young man's feet, whose name was Saul.** 59 **And they stoned Stephen, calling upon God, and saying, Lord Jesus, receive my spirit.** Saul, the Christians' enemy, would become their greatest Apostle. Acts 9:3 **And as he journeyed, he came near Damascus: and suddenly there shined round about him a light from heaven.**

I once had an employer who had, through error or stealth, refused to pay over three thousand dollars owed me. I was trying to collect while living on another continent. This financial setback made it hard for me and my young family. It was difficult, but at the time I forgave and handed the problem over to God. The next day a wonderful solution had come our way and we were fine.

When I moved back to Canada I was able to talk to the old employer and we resolved the debt that was owed to me. The bonus was that just arriving back into my country, the money was more than enough to get us going again. What looked bad three years earlier ended up being a savings account for our return. God is Good. Rom. 8:28 **And we know that all things work together for good to them that love God, to them who are the called according to His purpose.**

WISDOM IS STRENGTH

Proverbs 24:5 A wise man is strong; yea, a man of knowledge increases strength.

How-to books are a billion dollar industry. How to get things done right and prosperous at the same time. Change our bad habits into good ones, and change our character in three easy steps. The only how-to book that I know that will work continually and efficiently every time is the Bible. The word of the bible will help character development and our hearts change into what God created us to be. Rom. 10:17 **So then faith comes by hearing, and hearing by the word of God.**

Yes, you can get a lot of good help by reading and practising some of the theories and formulas that are written about in all the self-help monologues, but nothing can change a hard human heart like God's word. Nothing can keep us on the right track like the living word of God. John 8:32 **And ye shall know the truth, and the truth shall make you free.**

The word states that we get off track and need help when we start believing a different voice other than God's. Rom. 1:21 **Because that, when they knew God, they glorified him not as God, neither were thankful; but became vain in their imaginations, and their foolish heart was darkened. 22 Professing themselves to be wise, they became fools.** The smorgasbord of available beliefs that are dangled in front of us daily are so numerous that if we did not have our foundation in God's word and His word working in our hearts, we too would become casualties of false doctrine. Mark 13:22 **For false Christs and false prophets shall rise, and shall shew signs and wonders, to seduce, if it were possible, even the elect.**

I am not easily shocked but I had one of those jaw-dropping situations this week when I heard a person say "Better to reign in hell than serve in heaven." This person actually meant what he had just said. There was no amount of logic or spiritual reasoning that made sense to this lost person's mind or heart. How does a soul get to a place in their heart that actually believes this nonsense? Prov. 23:9 **Speak not in the ears of**

a fool: for he will despise the wisdom of thy words. Living and bound in foolishness is how a person starts to believe the lies and nonsense from the enemy of our soul. There is no wisdom nor strength at work in this man, because there is no belief of God to help him along the way even though God is waiting to help and bless if asked.

Prov. 24:5 **A wise man is strong; yea, a man of knowledge increases strength.** The more we know God, the stronger we get. You will notice that I did not say "The more we know about God, the stronger we get." Knowing Him and knowing about Him are two different relationships. The children of Israel knew about God, but Moses knew God personally. Psalm 103:7 **He made known his ways unto Moses, his acts unto the children of Israel.**

Someone might ask. "How do I get to know God and not just about Him?" Heb. 11:6 **But without faith it is impossible to please Him: for he that comes to God must believe that He is, and that He is a rewarder of them that diligently seek Him.** Faith in God's word is how we will get to know the one who wrote the living word so we can live in strength and victory.

Choosing the wisdom in the word of God is the growing strength we live in every day. Acts 17:28a **For in Him we live, and move, and have our being.**

Psalm 14:1a **The fool hath said in his heart, There is no God.** There are a lot of fools out there in the world. If you are growing in the strength of God's word, you may be the only bible these fools will ever read. What will they read from your life? Will they want some of the victories you are living? A wise person is strong in the Lord and will keep getting stronger because God is at work in them. You are an Epistle read of men. May the people be reading the story of Jesus. Amen.

WHAT DID YOU EXPECT?

Proverbs 23:18 For surely there is an end; and thine expectation shall not be cut off.

There is a growing number of people in the church who have stopped expecting anything from God, and therefore, there is no disappointment when nothing happens. This type of self-preservation relationship has become a rote and neutral existence that has no life in, or out, of it. As a matter of fact, this lack of expectation in their Christian walk has started to destroy the joy in their everyday lives. Rev. 3:15 **I know your deeds, that you are neither cold nor hot. I wish you were either one or the other.**

This type of Sunday madness can bring harm to our personal relationship with our loving God because the Lord is continually reaching out to our souls to expand His love within us. If there is no receptivity from our hearts, then how do we go forward? Mark 4:25 **And he said unto them, Take heed what ye hear: with what measure ye mete, it shall be measured to you: and unto** you that hear shall more be given. 25 For he that hath, to him shall be given: and he that hath not, from him shall be taken even that which he hath.

God is a living being and so are we. Life moves, breathes and feels in a constant forward motion. If life cannot stand still, then how can we stand inert and mute in a living body; the church? Acts 17:28a **For in him we live, and move, and have our being.** Many of us struggle in our faith when we have gone through trials that seem to be overwhelming. We are not the first ones to go through this. Jeremiah was fed up with the responsibility of the word in his life, but when he tried to stop the motion of the living word in his heart it was impossible not to be who God called him to be. Jer. 20:9 **Then I said, I will not make mention of Him, nor speak any more in His name. But His word was in mine heart as a burning fire shut up in my bones, and I was weary with forbearing, and I could not stay.**

Moses struggled with the feelings of his inability to provide meat for the large population. Moses was fed up to the point of sarcasm. Num. 11:12 **Have I conceived all this people? have I** begotten them, that thou should say unto me, carry them in thy bosom, as a nursing father bears the sucking child, unto the land which thou swarest unto their fathers?** Moses was basically saying, "When are you going to answer this prayer?" Then God answers. Num. 11:23 **Then the LORD said to Moses, "Has my arm lost its power? Now you will see whether or not my word comes true!"**

I could speak of Job, Hezekiah, Gideon and many others who had just wanted to shut it down and give up. The thing that always changed the circumstances were the words, "Then the LORD said!" This is the point: that God eventually comes through. Prov. 23:18 **For surely there is an end; and thine expectation shall not be cut off.** Giving up on prayer is not the answer to our prayers, because the Holy Spirit lives in us and He intercedes on our behalf all the time with prayer. Rom. 8:26 **Likewise the Spirit also helps our infirmities: for we know not what we should pray for as we ought: but the Spirit itself makes intercession for us with groanings which cannot be uttered.** Jesus, our Lord, who lives in our hearts, intercedes for us; therefore, we are constantly surrounded by prayer whether we want to pray or not. We need to accept by faith God's prayers that are prayed for us. Heb. 7:25 **Wherefore He is able also to save them to the uttermost that come unto God by Him, seeing He ever lives to make intercession for them.**

Our expectation will not be cut off because the Lord Jesus is working toward our victory. Jude 1:24 **Now unto him that is able to keep you from falling, and to present you faultless before the presence of his glory with exceeding joy.** The Godhead has put way too much into our eternal lives to leave us floundering around with a mediocre relationship. Half-hearted attempts at communication will not do. God desires all of our being and He has the right to ask for it. Thank you, Lord, for your constant pursuit of our lives. You are a good God.

SINNERS SIN

Proverbs 14:16 A wise man fears and departs from evil, But a fool rages and is self-confident.

What is all the hoopla about? Why are people raging rather than praying about government legislation allowing the different types of sinners to live out their sin. Sinners sin, that is what they do. Prayer changes things, not angry slogans. Honest love and intercession change hearts, not acrimonious debates. Sinners have always sinned and will always sin. If you would take a moment and remember your own lives before you asked Christ to be the Lord of your life, you will recall that you sinned a whole lot and that was the nature of your soul. Gal. 6:8 **For he that sows to his flesh shall of the flesh reap corruption; but he that sows to the Spirit shall of the Spirit reap life everlasting.**

Sinners are doing what they do best, they sin. This is why God asks us to pray for one another so that He can work His will within us. Phil. 2:13 **For it is God which works in you both to will**

and to do of His good pleasure. God asks us to pray for the government official for the same reason and more. 1Tim. 2:1 **I exhort therefore, that, first of all, supplications, prayers, intercessions, and giving of thanks, be made for all men; 2 For kings, and for all that are in authority; that we may lead a quiet and peaceable life in all godliness and honesty.**

Go ahead and write your government official if that is driving your mind right now, but don't spew out all your anger on them; rather, let them know that you are praying for them to do the best they can and that God would lead them in their decisions. If you do that then you will have fulfilled the word of God and put the official in God's hands to be judged righteously, just the way you would like God to judge you. Out of that heart action and obedience the peace of God will rule your heart and bring the peace of being able to live in peace and godliness.

What made Jesus different from the ministers in Israel when Jesus walked the earth? He loved them and people wanted to be around him. The Pharisees, Sadducees and Herodians had all taken political positions on righteousness and were trying to legislate holiness that they could not keep themselves. Jesus dealt with the true issues of the day. Sin was causing a rift between the people and their God. Jesus exposed this problem with the love of God. Acts 10:38 **God anointed Jesus of Nazareth with the Holy Spirit and power, and how He went around doing good and healing all who were under the power of the devil, because God was with Him.**

What has changed? We who are in Christ, are to be doing the same thing. We are to go around doing good and healing all who are under the power of the devil because God is with us. I don't think that means to post your seething hatred in the comment forums on Facebook and all the other media sites that are available to you. Remember, sinners sin. That is what they do. It is the Holy Spirit that will convict the world of righteousness, sin and judgment; not you. John 16:8 **And when he comes, he will convict the world of its sin, and of God's righteousness, and of the coming judgment.** My job is to love the sinner and hate the sin. My mission is to embrace the unlovable and hate the garments of their bondage. Jude 1:23 **Rescue others by**

snatching them from the flames of judgment. Show mercy to still others, but do so with great caution, hating the sins that contaminate their lives.

We were never called or asked by God to hate the sinner but only the sins that have corrupted this world. Just because a group of sinners vote to bring in an unrighteous law does not make the sin acceptable or a present truth in God's eyes. During Noah's lifetime, the whole earth voted on living in an existence of debauchery. Noah and God were the majority and what God said was the truth of the matter. It did not matter what laws the sinful had legislated; God's truth prevailed and will always prevail. Prov. 21:30 **There is no wisdom, no insight, no plan that can succeed against the LORD.**

Join me in praying for the people who think that by changing the laws to suit their sin of choice will make them happy and peacefully fulfilled. We know it won't. At the end of their empty war they will still need salvation and Christ will be there for them. Let us pray for our leaders who have very difficult jobs trying to appease all types of agendas inspired by the enemy of our soul.

We can do a lot more than feud on a media site. We can actually bring a real righteous change by doing what Christ has asked us to do and that is pray. Matt. 9:38 **So pray to the Lord who is in charge of the harvest; ask him to send more workers into his fields. 1Tim. 2:1 Therefore I exhort first of all that supplications, prayers, intercessions, and giving of thanks be made for all men, 2 for kings and all who are in authority, that we may lead a quiet and peaceable life in all godliness and reverence.** When we start to do this God will give us the strategy as to how to help the lost. God bless us all.

THE REAL PRISONERS

Proverbs 4:14 Do not set foot on the path of the wicked or walk in the way of evildoers.

Quote: Not all prisons have steel bars.

In 1980, while I was attending bible college in Australia, I ministered with a group called Broken Chains Prison Ministry out of Sydney. On most weekends, we went into the different prisons throughout New South Wales and brought with us a variety of rock bands and musos who were Christians and keen on helping in prison ministry. The musicians expressed their faith in Christ through their music and personal testimonies of God's goodness in their lives. We also provided the prisoners with Christian material they had requested that declared, "Jesus Christ is Lord," and He was their eternal hope if they chose to accept Him as their Lord and Savior. We were blessed to have had such favour of the Lord as we ministered week after week.

The interesting thing to me was that some of the prisoners who had become Christians while in prison and had a genuine relationship with the Lord were freer in their souls while in forced confinement, than a lot of the staff and guards who ran the security systems of the prisons. Even though the guards got to go home at night, a lot of them were bound in their souls because of the hatred they had for the criminals they oversaw. Who was really in prison? Who were the ones living in manacles? How was it possible to be able to go where and when you wanted on the outside of the prison walls, and yet, be more bound and chained than the Christian prisoners who were incarcerated?

Some of the guards were angry with us for ministering to the prisoner's spiritual needs. Their argument was that the prisoners were evil recidivists and they deserved to be locked up forever. In some cases, this may be true. However, God's word does say to visit the prisoner. Matt. 25:36 **I needed clothes and you clothed me, I was sick and you looked after me, I was in prison and you came to visit me.** What some of these guards did not realize was that they were becoming what they hated. They had inadvertently stepped on the same path the criminals were walking. Their anger towards the inmates had caused them to voice their personal judgements of justice, revenge, and punishment. They were becoming as hardheaded as some of the hardcore inmates. Prov. 4:14 **Do not set foot on the path of the wicked or walk in the way of evildoers.**

A person can be surrounded by the oppressive walls of a penitentiary, and the truth of God's word can free that soul from being bound by the invisible chains that many freed people are shackled to. John 8:32 **You will know the truth, and the truth will set you free.** People can become a prisoner of their own making by hanging on to hate, resentment, and unforgiveness. In some cases, they can also become more severe and harsher on themselves because they become their own jailers by not letting go of their hate.

Lately, we have heard of people who were once dependable and stable citizens falling into the deep holes of believing every conspiracy theory that comes their way. They become prisoners of all the secretive and dark information they have personally accumulated to prove every single event going on in life is an attack and scheme to destroy their way of life. The sad thing is, they end up destroying their own lives by their never-ending angry conversations that alienate everyone around them. Deeper and deeper they fall into a terrifying abyss until words like Illuminati, sanctioned killings, tracking devices, microchip-readers, and listening devices become the steel bars of their personal cage they now find themselves fighting from. Even if everything they said was a fact, how would they personally stop it all? How could they go around the world and expose and fix every conspiracy that is supposedly going on? This would be impossible to do.

Who are the real prisoners in life? Are they not the ones who are caged within their own bondage? The Apostle Paul wrote a large part of the New Testament from prison. Phil. 1:13 **So that it has become known throughout the whole imperial guard, and to everyone else, that my imprisonment is because I am in Christ.** Paul was a prisoner of the Roman Empire's system, but in his heart, Paul was the Lord's prisoner, and this knowledge allowed him inner freedom while in prison. He called himself a prisoner in the Lord, and this truth broke the chains of the world system Paul was ministering in. Eph.4:1a **Therefore I, the prisoner in the Lord, urge you to walk worthy.**

I'm not saying Paul had an easy time in prison. On the contrary, Roman prisons were brutal. What Paul had was the confidence in his Lord who could deliver him from all of the real treacherous conspiracies that were against him. 2Tim. 3:11 **Persecutions, sufferings—what kinds of things happened to me in Antioch, Iconium and Lystra, the persecutions I endured. Yet the Lord rescued me from all of them.** There were real plots to kill and control Paul. However, Paul didn't spend much time defending himself against all the accusations confronting him. He remained a free man by being a prisoner in Christ and letting God deal with his enemies.

We who are in Christ must be circumspect when it comes to all the trappings that could trick us into a jail of our own making. If we are going to be a prisoner of anything, then let it be a prisoner of gratefulness, kindness, generosity and love. Let us be prisoners in Christ so that we may remain free in our souls and heart. Amen and amen!

DEFERRED GRATIFICATION

Proverbs 25:28 A person without self-control is like a city with broken-down walls.

"I want it now!" is the mantra of the overindulgent generation. The idea of waiting and saving for something wanted has become so old-fashioned. Those of us who still do things that way are mocked as people who are not in touch with the times. Having self-control over one's spending habits is seen as a waste of time when all you have to do is get it now and pay later. Offers of easy money that should not be refused are promoted twenty-four-seven with the added enticement that says "You deserve it."

We live in an overcharged consumptive world where nothing is denied and no one seems to be happier with all they can get at the click of an icon or the swipe of a charge card. The Lord warned us of this treasure hunting attitude that can take a toll on our hearts. Matt. 6:19 **Do not store up for yourselves treasures on earth, where moths and vermin destroy, and where**

thieves break in and steal. 20 But store up for yourselves treasures in heaven, where moths and vermin do not destroy, and where thieves do not break in and steal.

No! I am not against shopping at the mall. As a matter of fact, the majority of the miracles in the new testament were manifested in the streets and marketplaces where Jesus and the apostles ministered. I am only thinking out loud as I watch people shuffling their way through their daily grind, looking for that thing that will bring joy and satisfaction to their souls. The assembly of the first mall is attended regularly with heartfelt dedication and the willingness to offer up hard-earned or borrowed money to the gods of glitz and glam seems to be done without thought.

Worshipers of the newest device line up for hours and sometimes days in order to get the product that will ordain the individual as acceptable in society. The rush to spend money they don't have on brand names not needed to impress people not liked is the doctrine numbingly followed. All this froth of activity in order to have a sense of self-worth while Jesus says to us all that the rest and gratification we are looking for is in

Him. Matt. 11:28 **Come to me, all you who are weary and burdened, and I will give you rest.**

There is nothing wrong with owning the latest device offered in the marketplace, but not at the cost of your personal peace and integrity. Counseling the young and old who are in debt to lenders of fast money has been heartbreaking. All they can think of is declaring personal bankruptcy and starting all over again. Therein is the problem. Starting all over again and not fixing the problem that got them to the point of bankruptcy in the first place. 2Tim. 3:7 **Always learning and never able to arrive at a knowledge of the truth.**

Deferred gratification is such a foreign idea to these indebted ones. When I bring it up in counsel they look at me as if I am an alien. Maybe I am an alien, but this alien is not in debt and hopefully has developed a sense of self-control in life. 1Pet. 2:11 **Beloved, I exhort you as aliens and sojourners, to abstain from fleshly desires, which war against your soul, 12 keep your conduct among the Gentiles honorable, so that when they speak against you as evildoers, they may see your good deeds and glorify God on the day of visitation.**

If you want to covet and cannot wait for the next thing, then covet the things of God. 1 Tim. 6:11 **But you, O man of God, flee from these things and pursue righteousness, godliness, faith, love, perseverance, and gentleness.** With the enthusiasm of the overnight shopper in line for the newest toy, how about lining up in God's presence for an evening of prayer and searching the scriptures for the answer needed in your life right now? Instead of spending money you do not have, why not spend some time with God finding out how to create wealth that will bring joy within the kingdom of God and to your life.

Work out a faith project with the Lord and see what He can do when God becomes your gratification in life. Use your life-given energy to become God's blessing in the world rather than another statistic of human failure because you just had to have it now! Become grateful for what you have and stop worrying that you will miss out. God is not finished with you. The Lord has you in the palm of his hand and is working a miracle in your life right now, so be at peace and be gratified in His love. Jude 1:24 **Now unto him that is** able to keep you from falling, and to present you faultless before the presence of his glory with exceeding joy, 25 To the only wise God our Saviour, be glory and majesty, dominion and power, both now and ever. Amen.

PART FOUR:

QUESTIONS FOR UNDERSTANDING

1. *What did you learn in this section of the book?*
2. *What surprised you the most?*
3. *What subject(s) spoke to your heart?*
4. *Did the material that you read help you understand the subject(s) more or less?*
5. *What topics are important to you? Why?*
6. *How do these articles relate to you?*
7. *After reading this section of the book, what will you change in your life?*

PART FIVE:

CHILDLIKE FAITH

Noticed, But Not Seen

Childlike faith is not childish faith. Childlike faith looks at who is making the promise, and who can be trusted to carry out the promise. We have The Almighty God making promises to us through His son Jesus. God can be trusted, and is worthy of our faith in Him because God is love.

CHILDLIKE FAITH

Proverbs 7:24 Now therefore, listen to me, my children; pay attention to the words of my mouth.

Childlike faith is not complicated, and this is why it works. You do not have to explain to a child the ten steps to receiving and six ways of affirming, plus three levels of asking God's favour to answer prayers. Children just ask, believe, then get on with playing. Now we who are supposed to be wise and full of the Holy Spirit tend to mess this simple process up with multiple steps and hoops to jump through to get God's attention, let alone answered prayer. Maybe this is why Christ wanted us to observe the simple faith of a child. Matt. 19:14 **But Jesus said, "Permit the little children, and do not forbid them to come to Me, for of such is the kingdom of the heavens."**

Matt. 18:3 **"Truly I tell you," He said, "unless you turn and become like children, you will never enter the kingdom of heaven.** Childlike faith is not to be mixed up with childish faith which is a presumptuous and foolish fatalism. 1Cor. 13:11b **I put aside childish things.** We are not to be childish and immature in our faith but rather we are to respond by believing what God says about our lives and situations in the same way a child believes when a parent lovingly explains certain facts about life that are going on around them.

The heart of God is moved by childlike faith because children have a simple confidence in the love that God has for them. 1John 5:14 **This is the confidence we have before Him: If we ask anything according to His will, He hears us. 15 And if we know that He hears whatever we ask, we know that we have what we have asked of Him.** God's will toward us is that we would be willing to believe the love God has for us and that we have a repentant heart toward Him. 2Pet. 3:9 **The Lord is not slack concerning His promise, as some count slackness, but is longsuffering toward us, not willing that any should perish but that all should come to repentance.** Childlike faith understands friendship with God because the child's heart is open to believing anything is possible.

At the wedding of Cana, the servants obeyed Mary with childlike faith by doing what Jesus told them to do. John 2:5 **"Do whatever He tells you,"** **his mother told the servants.** The servants may have been asked what they were doing filling six thirty-gallon clay pots with water. Their response would have been a simple, "Jesus said to do it." Blind Bartimaeus said without doubt when asked by Jesus what he wanted. "I want to see," was his response, and his eyes were opened. There does not seem to be much indecision when childlike faith is being used. Heb. 11:6 **Now without faith it is impossible to please God, since the one who draws near to Him must believe that He exists and that He rewards those who seek Him.**

In the Gospel of Mark, we read the story of the four men who carried a paralyzed man to Jesus on a stretcher. When they could not reach the Lord because the crowd was too large and was blocking the entrance, they went on top of the dwelling place where Jesus was ministering. They broke through the roof and lowered the man toward Jesus. The word records the Lord's reaction to their faith. Mark 2:5 **When Jesus saw**

their faith, He said to the paralyzed man, "Son, your sins are forgiven." When Jesus saw their faith, - is a powerful statement. What did Jesus see that so moved the Lord to have it recorded this way? The four men may have said, "If we can get him in front of Jesus, then he will be healed." A child would reason in the same fashion. Just like the woman who was afflicted with the issue of blood said, "If I can touch the edge of his garment, I will be healed!" These are statements that need no signs or course studies in faith.

We can all remember at some time, the Lord answering a prayer we simply asked to be met. We left the request at the altar of God's divine goodness. Like a child, we smiled and said, "Praise the Lord," when the answer came through on our behalf. In most cases, the answered prayer was beyond what we had asked or even thought possible. The joie de vivre we experienced was so exuberant that we knew the Lord had blessed us with His favour and love. Faith in God is just that, it is faith in the love God demonstrates toward us through our relationship with Him.

Sometimes, our misinterpretation as to what

we think faith is can cause all kinds of problems within our walk with the Lord, plus create division between our brothers and sisters in Christ. We can become childish in our reactions to what God is doing because we assume a misguided understanding of faith. God's word is the foundation of faith and from His word we approach God as His children. Prov. 7:24 **Now therefore, listen to me, my children; pay attention to the words of my mouth.** Childlike faith says, "Yes God, Your will be done according to Your word." May God's face shine on us and give us the desires of our heart, that we may be the blessing of the Lord He intended us to be. Have faith in God. Amen!

PROTECTED FROM OURSELVES

Proverbs 2:8 He guards the paths of the just and protects those who are faithful to him.

How many times has God come through for you, by protecting you from something you were the reason protection was needed? We see God coming to the rescue continually to help and protect people from their own dumb and nonsensical decisions. The Lord promised a saviour for Adam and Eve after they had sinned, resulting in salvation for anyone who chose God's gift of salvation through Christ. At another time, God sent a whale to pick up Jonah while he was running away in disobedience of the instructions God had given him. God is continually on guard and looking out for us. Isa. 52:12 **You will not leave in a hurry, running for your lives. For the LORD will go ahead of you; yes, the God of Israel will protect you from behind.**

I have recently been protected for two dumb things I did with my house and car keys. The other morning, I was looking for my keys and could not find them anywhere. I went out to the car to see if I had left them there. Then I noticed the keys in the outside door keyhole. The keys were cold from being there all night. Great burglar protection. Just leave the keys in the lock for anyone to use. Again, the other morning, while meeting friends at a restaurant, I left my keys in the car ignition with the doors unlocked. I only noticed the keys were missing as I was leaving the restaurant. Not a good car-theft deterrent. All I could say was, "Thank you, Lord, for protecting me from myself." Prov. 2:8 **He guards the paths of the just and protects those who are faithful to him.**

We try to control everything that goes on around us. We think we can keep on top of every aspect of our lives, but time and time again, we see that we come up short of the perfection and security we are trying to create. We even try to protect ourselves from the inevitability of death which is in God's control and domain. Eccl. 8:8 **None of us can hold back our spirit from departing. None of us has the power to prevent the day of our death. There is no escaping that obligation, that dark battle.**

And in the face of death, wickedness will certainly not rescue the wicked. We need God to protect us from our narcissistic belief that we have it all under control and that we are on top of it all. How deceived we can become, by not realizing that even our breath is lent to us by God. Isa. 2:22a **Put no more trust in a mere human, who has only the breath in his nostrils.**

I often look around and wonder how we, as a human race, have made it this far. We only have to watch the nightly news to see how messed up the people of this earth have become. We keep putting ourselves in danger of annihilation. Across the continents, we have nuclear missiles pointed at each other and hopefully, no one accidentally sets one off. This would definitely throw a spanner into our Nuclear Détente arrangements that are negotiated worldwide. I mean, just one accidental nuclear explosion could ruin our day. We certainly need God to deliver us from ourselves.

The Apostle Peter had made some bold statements about his love for Jesus. He boasted that he would die for the Lord, but as Jesus predicted, within hours, Peter had denied even knowing the Lord. Peter ran off in shame because of his cowardly behaviour. He needed protection from himself and only Jesus the forgiving Lord could restore the emotional and spiritual confidence Peter needed so he could repent and get back on the Lord's agenda. The Lord did warn Peter that he would be tested and when he came through it, to help his brothers in the Lord. Luke 22:31 **Simon, Simon, look out. Satan has asked to sift you like wheat. 32 But I have prayed for you that your faith may not fail. And you, when you have turned back, strengthen your brothers.**

Jesus sits at the right hand of the Father praying and interceding for each one of us. He prays that we fulfill what we have been created for and that the resurrection power of Christ keeps us walking in His righteousness. Rom. 8:34b **Christ Jesus is the one who died, but even more, has been raised; he also is at the right hand of God and intercedes for us.** Hopefully, we have the sense to not walk into the world's sludge and slurry that is off the path of the righteous. However, if we do miss the clear markings of the narrow road we are to travel on, we can count on the fact that God will protect us from ourselves and our foolish decisions. God has our eternal souls in His hands and will forgive us when we ask through faith in Christ.

Praise the Lord for He is so good. May we all give thanks for all the times our God has come through for us. Amen!

ALL I NEED

Proverbs 13:25 The righteous has enough to satisfy his appetite, but the stomach of the wicked is in need.

"All I need is you," booms out from the majority of songs coming through the speakers at the gym while working out. Sometimes, I find myself responding to whom these songs were written for. I end up saying, "Don't believe anything they say, it's all cheap infatuation." All I need is you, which is a common theme in so many songs, poems, and videos are available at any time and in all forms of artful communication. A constant declaration of - "All I need is you, and if I get you, we will be happy forever."

If we actually knew what we needed there would not be so much confusion in life. One thing we do need is each other. We need the love of our Heavenly Father and the fellowship of our brothers and sisters in the Lord. We need to lift each other up in prayer and honour one another in the sight of our Lord. Mark 12:30 **And you** must love the **LORD** your God with all your heart, all your soul, all your mind, and all your strength. 31 **The second is equally important: 'Love your neighbor as yourself.' No other commandment is greater than these.**

When we are at peace with who we are in Christ, our hearts will be able to believe in the will of God for our lives, and we will learn to be content throughout life. Phil. 4:11 **I don't say this out of need, for I have learned to be content in whatever circumstances I find myself.** What we really need is what God has for us. Phil. 4:19 **But my God shall supply all your need according to his riches in glory by Christ Jesus.** Yes, we have to make our requests known to God, and we have to trust that the Lord will guide us in our prayers that are according to His will. God's will toward us is favour and soul-fulfilling eternal life. God wants to help us become blessings in this lost world.

There is an account in the Book of Second Kings that explains how God understands our needs in this troubled life. The Lord knows we need deliverance from our own unwise choices. One of Elisha's prophets died leaving his widow in a desperate situation. She was broke and her son was about to go into an arrangement of forced labour because of the outstanding debts that could not be paid. This woman was alone, without resources, in debt, and spiritually crushed because of the weight she was under. This sounds no different than so many people's stories today. I'm sure she had said on a few occasions, "All I need is HELP!!"

Help did come to her, but most likely not in the way she thought her needs would be met. We often have an agenda for God and instructions as to how He can help us. However, God knows how to meet our needs so that there is no doubt where the help came from. 2Kings 4:2 **Elisha replied to her, "How can I help you? Tell me, what do you have in your house?" "Your servant has nothing there at all," she said, "except a small jar of olive oil."** God may ask, what do you have in your house? You may feel that you have nothing because of the stress you are under. But if we take a moment and answer God by offering Him our heart, He will be able to use what we offer as a way out of our mess.

Elisha's instructions were clear and precise.

2Kings 4:3 Elisha said, "Go around and ask all your neighbors for empty jars. Don't ask for just a few. 4 Then go into your house with your sons and shut the door behind you. Pour olive oil from your flask into the jars, setting each one aside when it is filled. The instruction to close the door was key. Could you imagine the neighbours from whom she had borrowed the jars looking in on her activity? If they could see into this private miracle taking place behind the closed door they would have had all kinds of suggestions of how to make the miracle even better than God had given her. The Lord was protecting her faith from being tainted by all the pseudo advice and religious opinions that would be proclaimed out loud.

God knows our needs and will bless us, not because we are in need, but rather because He is so good. Not only did God help the widow pay off her debts, but also made it possible for her to start an oil business that would take care of her and her children into the future. **2Kings 4:7 Then she came and told the man of God. And he said, Go, sell the oil, and pay thy debt, and live thou and thy children of the rest.**

The God of more than enough came through for her. She was able to live on the extra oil God had provided. Prov. 13:25a **The righteous has enough to satisfy his appetite.**

All I need is God working in my life and all I need to do is submit to the work He is doing in my heart. The Lord will provide what we need to get through this life and well on our way into our eternal life. Praise the Lord for His goodness toward us all. Amen!

WHAT DO YOU WANT?

Proverbs 17:27 He that hath knowledge spares his words: and a man of understanding is of an excellent spirit.

Knowing when to speak, and better yet, what to say at the appropriate time in order to bring healing to any soul, is a gift. We read in the book of Daniel that he was such a man. When Daniel was summoned before the greatest king on earth at that time, Daniel did not jabber. He answered all questions with clarity and accuracy so that no one was in doubt as to what Daniel had said by the Spirit of God. Dan. 6:3 **Then this Daniel was preferred above the presidents and princes, because an excellent spirit was in him.**

Our lives are inundated with a constant barrage of words all day long. In all this daily noise, was anything said that gave us life? Job 6:24 **Teach me, and I will hold my tongue: and cause me to understand wherein I have erred.** Is it possible to even have our words count for something of value within this present day flood of social media extravaganza?

1Sam. 3:19 **And Samuel grew, and the LORD was with him, and did let none of his words fall to the ground.** Samuel had acquired by the Spirit of God the skill of having his words count, and we need this today.

Even when many of us are in prayer, our words are all over the map with a lot of humm, ahem, yeaaah, haah, and so on. We don't seem to know what we want when approaching our God for our lives. Yet the Word has said that if we ask, we will have our requests heard. 1John 5:14 **And this is the confidence that we have in Him, that, if we ask any thing according to His will, He hears us: 15 And if we know that He hear us, whatsoever we ask, we know that we have the petitions that we desired of Him.**

With this kind of grace favouring us, why then are we mumbling our way through prayer? The Lord is constantly encouraging us to ask, and be clear about it. Matt. 7:7 **Ask, and it shall be given you; seek, and ye shall find; knock, and it shall be opened unto you: 8 For every one that asks receives; and he that seeks finds; and to him that knocks it shall be opened.**

Some of you might be saying at this point, now come on "BROTHER," it is not that simple. I think it can be, because when we read the story of blind Bartimaeus in Mark 10:46-52, we read that after Bartimaeus had the Lord's attention and is standing before Jesus, this account is recorded. Mark 10:51 **So Jesus answered and said to him, "What do you want Me to do for you?" The blind man said to Him, "Rabboni, that I may receive my sight." 52 Then Jesus said to him, "Go your way; your faith has made you well." And immediately he received his sight and followed Jesus on the road.**

Jesus said, "WHAT DO YOU WANT?" The blind man said, "I WANT TO SEE!" There was no preamble or religious posturing. It was said by faith "I want to see," and that was that. At no time did the blind man mumble, jabber, and complain about how hard it had been being blind. He did not tell the Lord all the things he did not want. His prayer was clear as to what he wanted, and that was his sight.

No wonder the Scriptures say he followed Jesus after his miracle, because the first glorious sight that entered his eyes was the creator

Himself. Wow! I am inspired by this Scripture. It has calmed my heart to pray with peace and to ask what I want in Him. Job 6:8 **Oh that I might have my request; and that God would grant me the thing that I long for!**

The Lord is not asking us to perform the prayer. He is asking us to believe in Him through prayer. Prov. 17:27 **He that hath knowledge spares his words: and a man of understanding is of an excellent spirit.** A few words of faith prayed to our Heavenly Father avails much, in Jesus name!

THE BEST VERSION OF YOU

Proverbs 15:3 The eyes of the LORD are everywhere, observing the wicked and the good.

1Sam. 16:7 **But the LORD said to Samuel, "Do not look on his appearance or on the height of his stature, because I have rejected him. For the LORD sees not as man sees: man looks on the outward appearance, but the LORD looks on the heart.** If we could see ourselves from God's point of view, we would be utterly amazed at who God knows us to be in Christ Jesus. If we want to know the best version of who we are, then we will have to commune with the Lord. We will not find God's eternal version of ourselves in a self-help book, self-improvement app, or on the pages of a glossy magazine. We will only find out who we are in the presence of the Lord.

The Lord created us and weaved our DNA out of His infinite vision of who we are. God thought of us individually, and here we are, living and breathing souls. Psalm 139:13 **For**

you formed my inward parts; you knitted me together in my mother's womb. The devil sees the worst version of our lives because all he ever sees is the evil that is on the earth. God, on the other hand, can see the best possible version of our hearts because the Lord can see our eternity in Christ. The Lord can direct and woo our souls because He created them, and knows exactly what will inspire us. Yes, we still have the free will to choose whether we will follow God. The Lord's advantage is that He created the abilities and giftings within our souls and He knows our purpose for living. Therefore, the Lord can direct us with honest love and devotion toward our well-being.

Satan can only tempt, abuse, and deceive us into believing that we are less than who God says we are. The devil tempts us with sin, abuses us with depression, and deceives us with lies so that we do not believe the version of who God says we are in Christ. Satan has to beguile our hearts because he has no real power or say over our lives. Therefore, the devil must con us into relinquishing the authority God has given us, plus he is jealous of the love God has for us.

This jealousy causes him to act out in continual tantrums like an evil petulant child as he breaks everything God declared as good. Satan intends to destroy the true version of our life's purpose with distortions and fabricated lies. John 8:44b **When he lies, it is consistent with his character; for he is a liar and the father of lies.**

The devil's focus on us is far too intense, and therefore, we have to be more than the mess he says we are. If it is true that we are all the terrible things Satan says we are, then why does he have to keep reinforcing the bullying narrative that he spews over and over again? The reality is that we are eternally secure in our saviour's hands, but Satan's time is short. Rev. 12:12b **For the devil has come down to you, having great wrath, because he knows that he has a short time.** It is not our time that is short, it is the enemy of our soul's time that is coming to an end, and he is violently opposed to our expressing and living with the love of God. Even though Satan pretends to be an angel of light, we will never get the best version of who we are from his ugly dark heart. It is impossible for Satan to love and have joy. How pathetic he is.

Why is the joy of the Lord our strength? Because in God's presence there is joy forevermore. The joy, peace, and love that emanates from God rains on us, who are the apple of His eye. Psalm 17:8 **Keep me as the apple of Your eye; hide me under the shadow of Your wings.** We cannot come away from the presence of the Lord without being transformed, revived, and inspired to be the person God says we are in Christ. If you want food, you grow it or go to a food store. If you want gasoline for your car, you go to a gas station. If you want to fly to another country, you go to the airport and take a flight. If you want real love, you go to the Godhead who is love.

God knows every person who exists by name and every situation we are in, whether good or bad. Prov. 15:3 **The eyes of the LORD are everywhere, observing the wicked and the good.** Those who are in Christ can grow into the version of who God says they are. If we want to be the best version of ourselves, then our Heavenly Father is the only one who knows the beginning from the end of our entire lives. The Lord has the blueprint to the very DNA we are knitted with. We do not need to go to a counterfeit blowhard liar like Satan, who claims to know what we need. No, Saints. We go to the Lord of mercy, the author and finisher of our faith, to be the best version of who we are in Christ. Amen!

WHO DO YOU TRUST?

Proverbs 25:19 Confidence in an unfaithful man in time of trouble is like a broken tooth, and a foot out of joint.

How many cult leaders have led thousands astray to a Christ-less end? The people who followed had put their trust in an unfaithful, yet charismatic, and maybe even sincere man. Within the last four decades, there have been some terrible tragedies with the likes of Jim Jones with the People's Temple cult whose legacy ends with, "The Jonestown Massacre."

There was David Koresh who brought his followers to a fiery end, and their legacy reads, "The Waco, Texas, Massacre." Sadder still was Marshall Applewhite who was leading a UFO doomsday following known as Hale-Bopp and Heaven's Gate cult. Their legacy was just as tragic and similar to all the other victims who had put their trust in an unfaithful and finite man. Heaven's Gate ending headlines read, "Suicide of 39 Members of the Heaven's Gate Cult." Prov.

14:12 **There is a way which seems right unto a man, but the end thereof are the ways of death.**

These examples are not extreme as there have been many others all over the world and their ending was just as fatal. In whom we put our trust is important. Jesus says in John 14:6 **Jesus saith unto him, I am the way, the truth, and the life: no man comes unto the Father, but by me.**

This word can be taken with full belief and heartfelt trust because Jesus is still a faithful Saviour and Lord. Christ gave His life for us so that we would not have to resort to self-flagellation and suicidal-beliefs in order to be accepted by God.

I am sometimes asked, "How can I have confidence in my spiritual leaders and know if they are not wolves in sheep's clothing?" We are given a criteria to look for in Heb. 13:7 **Remember them which have the rule over you, who have spoken unto you the word of God: whose faith follow, considering the end of their conversation. 8 Jesus Christ the same yesterday, and today, and forever.**

Plainly stated, the word is saying when it is all said and done, look for these facts. Are the words and actions of your pastors, teachers, and spiritual leaders saying Jesus Christ is the same yesterday, today, and forever? Is the end result of your pastor's leading saying this very thing about our Lord Jesus? Are your spiritual leaders' lives living and saying that Jesus is Lord? If so, then follow them with the leading of the Holy Spirit, while remembering that your leaders are also being changed by the Lord as they grow in Christ throughout their lives.

We can also trust God's care for us because He says that we will know the hearts of our pastors by the fruit in their lives. Matt. 7:16a **Ye shall know them by their fruits.** Prov. 18:21 **Death and life are in the power of the tongue: and they that love it shall eat the fruit thereof.**

If you have been graced by God with wonderful leadership as I have, then we need to give a collective shout of gratitude to our Lord and Saviour. To be able to find faithful men and women who honor the call of God in their lives, in this day and age, is a precious commodity in our era of selfish-frivolousness.

With thanksgiving, we should bless and pray for our church leaders that they continue in the faith with Christ as their plumb line. Eph. 4:11 **And he gave some, apostles; and some, prophets; and some, evangelists; and some, pastors and teachers; 12 For the perfecting of the saints, for the work of the ministry, for the edifying of the body of Christ: 13 Till we all come in the unity of the faith, and of the knowledge of the Son of God, unto a perfect man, unto the measure of the stature of the fullness of Christ.**

As we all attend our congregational meetings this week, let us make a special effort to thank our pastors and church leaders for their love and dedication to Christ. Amen.

ESTABLISHED IN THOUGHT

Proverbs 16:3 Commit thy works unto the LORD, and thy thoughts shall be established.

There is some confusion in the body of Christ when it comes to knowing what to do to bring about the kingdom of God or just knowing what to do next. There is a smorgasbord of ideas that over time prove to have nothing to do with God or His kingdom, and we wonder where we missed the signs along the way. I believe that when we find out who we are in Christ, knowing what to do will merge alongside with who we are and guide us into what we should be doing. 1Cor. 2:12 **Now we have received, not the spirit of the world, but the spirit which is of God; that we might know the things that are freely given to us of God.**

God knows us inside and out and He also knows what we can and cannot do. Matt. 25:14 **And unto one he gave five talents, to another two, and to another one; to every man according to his several ability.** We get things mixed up when we start separating our lives from the vision that has been revealed in our heart. The assignment that God has impressed upon our spirits to get done within the kingdom of God somehow finds itself over there somewhere as an abstract idea, while we are over here wondering how it will be accomplished.

Being now separate from God's vision, we think that the vision is a God thing and I am out of my depth and ability, because I am just a congregant who works at a convenience store for a living. What could I do with a kingdom vision? I am over here and the pastor and his crew of anointed-ones are over there doing the God thing. There ends up being a disconnect in how to go about doing what it takes to get kingdom business done.

Is there still this (great gulf fixed) between clergy and parishioners in this day and age? Absolutely, and I feel the gulf is getting wider. It can start to feel like there is no way to get across the perceived chasm. Luke 16:26 **And beside all this, between us and you there is a great gulf fixed: so that they which would pass from hence to you cannot; neither can they pass to**

us, that would come from thence.

Is this some kind of blame game? No, it is the result of all the misunderstood teachings of life purpose, dream fulfillment, walk out your passion, or "Become the greatest in your field" teachings that have become non-affect or commonplace. Statements like, "What God wants for your life is this and that," as if they actually knew what God wants for each personal life.

We can find out what God wants for our lives by reading and meditating on His word and being led by the Holy Spirit in a day by day relationship. But grandiose generalized statements of (what God wants) can causes people to stop listening because most of what is being said has never come to pass or appears out of reach because it seemed like exclusivism.

It turned out to be spiritual fluff or a cheap version of a magic show held in church. Matt. 7:21 **Not every one that saith unto me, Lord, Lord, shall enter into the kingdom of heaven; but he that does the will of my Father which is in heaven.** I am not saying, "Do not read the very good and well-written material on purpose, vision, passion, and spiritual dreams." I read as much as I can to help me be a better servant of Christ and to know what is available to help improve my walk with the Lord. What I am saying is read the word of God first, and more often, so that we know when we are reading the self-help books they are actually confirming what we know in our spirits because it is the same thing the Spirit of God has said to our hearts. Otherwise it is just a lot of theory on what God might be saying. Prov. 16:3 **Commit thy works unto the LORD, and thy thoughts shall be established.**

We need our thoughts established. When our thoughts are established we know what to do because our work is committed to the Lord and He establishes the work and how to get it done. Sometimes it is as easy as reading the instructions (the bible) and doing what it says. We can get overwhelmed by all the Christian literature, events, conferences and television, plus all the CD offers that will change our lives forever by just sending in a small gift plus shipping and handling.

All these helps are needed and do help but, what has God been saying to our souls? Isa. 30:21 **And thine ears shall hear a word behind thee, saying, This is the way, walk ye in it, when**

ye turn to the right hand, and when ye turn to the left. When you do not know what to do, then do what you know. The events and struggles in our lives are facts, but the word of God is truth. What does the word of God say about our everyday life? Stay in the word of God, no matter how disappointed you might get or overwhelmed by the feelings of life itself.

There is a day and time of deliverance and God will prove Himself faithful to each one of us. Commit your work and daily living, by faith, unto the Lord so that your thoughts can be established in Christ. God bless you.

ARE YOU IN TROUBLE?

Proverbs 11:8 The righteous is delivered out of trouble, and the wicked comes in his stead.

Someone said, "If your memories are bigger than your dreams then you are in trouble."

Are you in trouble? Have you stopped dreaming? Are you sitting around remembering the old days because you are stuck in neutral? If so, then maybe you have given up on the promises of God that encourage us to dream for better lives in Him. Psalm 103:2 **Bless the LORD, O my soul, and forget not all his benefits.**

There are so many voices out there calling people away to exotic tantalizing alternatives that our God-given dreams can get clogged up with static interruption causing us to falter in bewilderment. Take heart, saints. Some of us might have fallen but we can get up and move forward because the word of the Lord says that our steps are ordered by the Lord. Psalm 37:23 **The steps of a good man are ordered by the LORD: and he delights in his way. 24 Though**

he fall, he shall not be utterly cast down: for the LORD upholds him with his hand.

That's right, we don't have to stay down and become a casualty or a statistic of failure within the world's system. Maybe some of your dreams and goals have been set on hold because of all the unseen events taking place in your life right now. Perhaps you have fallen down and feel like you cannot get up. Be assured the Lord is holding you up from falling into a mess, even though you might have caused the mess. Prov. 24:16 **For a just man falls seven times, and rises up again: but the wicked shall fall into mischief.**

The fact that you have fallen does not mean you have to stay in that place of despair and loss. We can say like the apostle Paul in Phil. 3:13 **No, dear brothers and sisters, I have not achieved it, but I focus on this one thing: Forgetting the past and looking forward to what lies ahead.** If you find yourself in trouble that was inflicted by others or self-made, then make a conscious effort to leave the troubles behind and do as Paul says, "Forgetting the past and looking forward to what lies ahead."

What dreams are in your heart that might

be alive but dormant? God created us with the ability to create, design, invent and go forward in the inspiration of the Holy Spirit bringing life and wonder to this fallen world. Even though we stumble and sometimes utterly fall does not mean we have lost our gifting or calling. God forbid we think that way. God encourages us to get up, repent, restore and move forward toward the blessed hope that lies before us in Christ. Psalm 43:5 **Why art thou cast down, O my soul? and why art thou disquieted within me? hope in God: for I shall yet praise him, who is the health of my countenance, and my God.**

The prodigal son was in trouble caused by his own choices. Sitting by the pigsty discouraged, depressed and dreamless, he decides to return to his father's home hoping for mercy. Luke 15:20 **And he arose, and came to his father. But when he was yet a great way off, his father saw him, and had compassion, and ran, and fell on his neck, and kissed him.** When the son returns, he finds out that it is not just his father's home but still his own home and he is welcome. His sonship is restored with a feast of grandeur and delight. Isn't it interesting that the son's steps that were ordered by the Lord led him back to his father who loved him?

Our heavenly Father is looking for us on the horizon of His love, wanting us to come home, and resume dreaming God's dreams for our lives. With the Lord's calling and gifting fully restored within us, we will help usher in the kingdom of God and all the blessings that come with it.

Are you in trouble? Come home to the Father who has set a plate at the dinner table for you. There are delightful and tasty blessings awaiting you that can help you turn your life into a miracle you never thought possible. Psalm 34:8 **Taste and see that the LORD is good; blessed is the one who takes refuge in him.** Come and dream a dream again. Don't believe things are impossible, because with God all things are possible. You might say to me, "You don't understand. My sins are so many. I am beyond redemption." Not so! All sins have been paid for in full by the blood of Jesus.

Just start heading home to the Father and He will meet you with love and open arms full of the help you need. 1 Cor. 10:13 **The temptations in your life are no different from what others**

experience. And God is faithful. He will not allow the temptation to be more than you can stand. When you are tempted, he will show you a way out so that you can endure. Are you in trouble? Ask God for a dream and a vision for your life. Blessings.

REAL PEACE

Proverbs 16:7 When a man's ways please the LORD, He makes even his enemies to be at peace with him.

Someone said, "If your inner mind is not deceived, your outer actions won't be wrong."

There are a lot of peace talks these days and the more of these photo-ops we see as peace agreements are signed, the more skeptical we become that the peace will hold or that the one's signing has any ability to assure a positive outcome of any kind. Is peace just the absence of war? If all wars were to stop overnight, would that be real peace? That is what we have come to believe in this fractious and often tumultuous world.

A government official stands up and declares all is well now because the war has died down and there are not as many casualties; therefore, peace looks promising. Although this type of peace is necessary to survive on this planet it is not what Jesus meant when He said He would give us His peace. John 14:27 **Peace I leave with you,**

my peace I give unto you: not as the world gives, give I unto you. Let not your heart be troubled, neither let it be afraid.

We know that peace is God's will for mankind because the first thing said at the birth of Jesus by the angel of the Lord was a declaration of peace toward all men on this earth. Luke 2:14 **Glory to God in the highest, and on earth peace, good will toward men.** Everyone is looking for some kind of peace. Peace and quiet is a commodity sought after by overworked and stressed people the world over. Big amounts of money are spent daily for that peaceful getaway where peace and relaxation are guaranteed.

The reality of that peace package upon return from the peaceful holiday to the real world is that the stressed life starts all over again. Gated communities are sold the world over as peaceful homes, settings and landscapes so that the occupants can live in a state of perpetual peace from the ugly outside world. Yet real peace is not found in the surrounding wall of an estate. Eze. 13:10 **Because they lead my people astray, saying, "Peace," when there is no peace, and because, when a flimsy wall is built, they**

cover it with whitewash.

Peace is not a commodity or something possessed through purchases of endless stuff. Real peace comes through the person of Jesus, the Price of Peace. When war, gang shootouts and revenge killings stop, there is an uneasy ceasefire or détente because the skirmish can start right up again with one insult or slight. When real peace is established in the hearts and minds of the people who have accepted Jesus' eternal peace, the result of using the Lord's peace as a standard brings real choices of reconciliation and forgiveness rather than revenge and another round of warfare. Phil. 4:7 **And the peace of God, which transcends all understanding, will guard your hearts and your minds in Christ Jesus.**

As the scripture says, God's peace is guarding our hearts and minds. One of God's names is Peace. Judges 6:24a **Then Gideon built an altar there unto the LORD, and called it Jehovah Shalom.** Why on earth would we look to politicians for peace when the God who is peace lives within us? The most man and government can provide for humanity is a precarious peace that is basically the absence of war. Is that a good thing? Yes, absolutely, we will take it. Who wants to live in a Syrian war-type of mayhem year after year?

God's peace will give us a faith-filled boldness that can move mountains and extend grace to people who have lost their way in life. Being children in the Lord's kingdom, it is His desire that we live, promote, and bring the Lord's peace to every corner of the world. Let us start in our own homes. Matt. 5:9 **Blessed are the peacemakers, for they will be called children of God. Amen!**

Norm Sawyer

FOR SUCH A TIME AS THIS

Proverbs 4:18 But the path of the just is like the shining sun, that shines ever brighter unto the perfect day.

Esther 4:14b **Who knows, perhaps you have come to your royal position for such a time as this.**

There is a reason why we are presently alive and living on this earth. When we consider the odds of making it to this day and still breathing to tell about it, we must recognize the abundant grace at work on our behalf. In my own family, my younger brother passed away at a young age and I have already lived longer in years than my grandfather did before he passed away.

Why has there been such favor and blessing of years given to me? We just have to read and watch the news to know that if we are alive and well, we should be most grateful. With all the wars, earthquakes, floods, texting and driving, hurricanes, hailstorms and catastrophes going on a regular basis, we are sure blessed to be alive.

244

Job 14:5 **A person's days are determined; You have decreed the number of his months and have set limits he cannot exceed.**

We are alive in spite of all the poisons in the atmosphere, prescription drugs leaching and polluting our drinking water supplies, plus the numerous artificial flavoring, preservatives and toxins in so many processed foods. It is a wonder that we are still moving along with purpose and vision. All I can say is "Wow, God is good to us and thank you Lord for keeping us well."

Like the Psalmist I also wonder why I am still alive and marvel at the grace God has shown me through the years. Psalm 8:3 **When I consider thy heavens, the work of thy fingers, the moon and the stars, which thou hast ordained; 4 What is man, that thou art mindful of him? and the son of man, that thou visit him?** It is no accident or coincidence that we are still here being guided by God's wisdom and hand.

Some people muse and say that they should have been born in another time or period in history. No, you were born for such a time as this. God has put within each one of us the ability and tools needed to meet the extreme challenges facing mankind at this time in our history. We were on God's mind when He thought of what would be needed in this world for our appointed time of life. Jer. 1:5a **Before I formed you in the womb I knew you, before you were born I set you apart.**

We were created for such a time as this period in our history. We are to go forward with the plan God has put within our hearts because the world needs that plan now. You do not have to go televise the plan nationally; you just have to step out in your own family, church, workplace, and neighbourhood.

We are often the miracle someone needs. If you have the ability to teach, then teach the next generation to get a hold of God with honest fervor. If you can dance, then teach someone to dance. If you can sing, then sing for some old lonely souls who need an uplifting moment in their day because you were born for such a time as this. Use what God has given you for the glory of God and the expansion of His kingdom.

God has given everyone talents according to their capability of managing them. Matt. 25:15 **And unto one he gave five talents, to another two,**

and to another one; to every man according to his several ability; and straightway took his journey. It does not matter if someone is more talented than you are because if they do not use the talent they have for good or even bring it out into the open, then what good is it? Don't do what the lazy servant did; burying his God-given abilities. If you do that, then at the end of life you will bemoan the fact that you never really lived a full-hearted life. You want to hear the Lord say, "Well done faithful servant", and not Matt. 25:26a **But the master replied, 'You wicked and lazy servant!**

One of the tricks the enemy of our soul uses is to say that the time is not right in order to delay, discourage and damage our life purpose and vision. The time is now and the season has come because there has never been so many opportunities to be a voice for God on this earth. Eccl. 3:1 **There is a time for everything, and a season for every activity under the heavens.**

There are more ways to communicate the vision and plan God has put in our heart than ever before in history. At the touch of a keyboard or any communication device, we can give out our God-inspired message to multiple people at the same time and reach areas of the earth that were in times past unreachable. Step out with the gift you have and see what the Lord can do with anyone who is willing to be used of God. Your time is now. You have been created for such a time as this.

PART FIVE:

QUESTIONS FOR UNDERSTANDING

1. *What did you learn in this section of the book?*
2. *What surprised you the most?*
3. *What subject(s) spoke to your heart?*
4. *Did the material that you read help you understand the subject(s) more or less?*
5. *What topics are important to you? Why?*
6. *How do these articles relate to you?*
7. *After reading this section of the book, what will you change in your life?*

Norm Sawyer

ABOUT THE AUTHOR

I have been in Christian ministry in one form or another for over forty years. In 1980 I attended Commonwealth Bible College in Katoomba, New South Wales, Australia. At that time I was involved in prison ministries, preaching on the radio in a small town, and church-related works of all kinds. I have taught bible college courses and also have been involved in personal discipleship training. God has blessed me all along the way. Now I have the opportunity to write down what was experienced throughout the years. The Lord has blessed me with sound and forthright material to write a series of Christian devotionals. I have lived the testimonies on these pages and can attest to the fact that God is so faithful and good. My hope is that your soul will be enriched as you read this book. God bless you.

CONNECT WITH NORM

Connect with Norm at Norm Sawyer's Blog
www.sirnorm.com

www.ingramcontent.com/pod-product-compliance
Lightning Source LLC
Chambersburg PA
CBHW070346090426
42733CB00009B/1300